Presentations as Performance

A Professional's Guide to Better Speaking

Richard Benjamin Crosby

NEW FORUMS

NEW FORUMS PRESS INC.

Published in the United States of America
by New Forums Press, Inc.1018 S. Lewis St.
Stillwater, OK 74074
www.newforums.com

Library of Congress Cataloging-in-Publication Data Pending

This book may be ordered in bulk quantities at discount from New Forums Press, Inc., P.O. Box 876, Stillwater, OK 74076 [Federal I.D. No. 73 1123239]. Printed in the United States of America.

ISBN 10: 1-58107-341-0
ISBN 13: 978-1-58107--341-6

Table of Contents

Introduction:

The Failure of Demosthenes

Demosthenes is regarded by historians of rhetoric as one of the best orators in history.

The greatest orator in history started out as a failure. Demosthenes of ancient Athens was well-schooled in law, business, and politics. So reliable was his learning that wealthy Athenian citizens who needed to defend themselves in the courts paid him to write their legal arguments and speeches. When Demosthenes found himself embroiled in a legal dispute of his own, however, he encountered a problem. Though his legal knowledge was impressive, his speaking talent was dismal.

As Plutarch describes the situation, Demosthenes exhibited a "strange and uncouth style, which was cumbered with long sentences and tortured with formal arguments to a most harsh and disagreeable excess. Besides, he had, it seems, a weakness in his voice, a perplexed and indistinct utterance and a shortness of breath."[1] Repulsed by his deficiencies, the assembly refused to even hear him. The world's future greatest orator covered his head in shame and began to walk home.

But a chance encounter along the way changed history. A man named Satyrus noticed Demosthenes skulking off and decided to intervene. An actor by training, Satyrus knew that the difference between failure and success in public speaking was a matter of performance and that, with a few pointers on "mien and gesture," anyone, including Demosthenes, could be transformed from failing to flourishing. Satyrus coupled his pointers with a small demonstration; and just like that, Demosthenes recognized that becoming a highly skilled speaker was "a small matter" only requiring practice in "enunciation and delivery."[2] Straightaway, Demosthenes built an underground study where he could rehearse his newfound skills privately in front of a mirror. He practiced speaking with pebbles in his mouth to minimize his speech impediment. He shaved the hair from half his head to avoid the temptation to leave his practice space. When he did emerge above ground, he practiced speaking on the beach next to the crashing waves in order to force himself to speak with greater volume and clarity. He also recited verses during long runs in order to improve his breathing capacity.

Demosthenes had learned that effective speaking is not a matter of natural-born talent or abstract knowledge but a matter of practice and performance. The remainder of his illustrious career was spent delivering innumerable public speeches defending the city of Athens against the incursions of Philip of Macedon and Alexander the Great. By the end of his life, he was regarded as a renowned orator and national hero. The people of Athens honored him with a golden crown in life and a brass statue in death. To this day, his speech "On the Crown" is considered a world masterpiece. It is fitting that an actor should receive the credit for Demosthenes's turnaround. Though he possessed deep learning, Demosthenes had lacked the ability to *deliver*. Not surprisingly, the famous Roman orator Quintilian reported that when asked later in life what the three most important elements of public speaking were, Demosthenes responded, "Delivery! Delivery! Delivery!"[3]

This small volume presumes the reader knows something but wants only to communicate it well. Fortunately, reasonable people do not expect their peers to be as eloquent as Demosthenes. The audience for this book is more modest, consisting of professionals, academics, teachers and their students, and perhaps regular members of the public. Such people are not looking for tear-jerking testimonies or soaring sermons. A professional audience simply wants someone who can communicate with competence and clarity. While this skill requires a certain level of performativity, it is something anyone can achieve. Some basic instruction and practice are all one requires.

It is worth it, too. Survey after survey reinforces a familiar finding: the top employers are looking for people who have formal and interpersonal communication skills—often called "soft skills"—more urgently than they are looking for anyone else. One recent survey by corporate recruiters with the Graduate Management Admission Council (GMAC) shows that the most valued proficiencies for MBAs are the following: "oral communication," "listening skills," "written communication," and "presentation skills." These four skills are not merely *in* the top ten; they make up four of the top five, ahead of "drive," "integrity," "ability to follow a leader," "quantitative analysis," "strategic vision," "technology," "language skills," "managing," "core business knowledge," and more. But this survey was designed mainly for MBAs. What about other professions? The US Bureau of Labor Statistics performed a data analytics study based on skills "wanted" across a massive range of job openings. At the very top of the list are "oral and written communication skills," ahead of "work independently," "motivated," "dependability," "work ethics," and "team-oriented." The study also reveals that when asked "which skills they rely on most," workers put "interpersonal skills" and "good written and spoken communication skills" at the top of the list.[4] Other studies, from the American Institute of Certified Public Accountants to the Department of Education, Science, and Training, come to the very same or a very similar conclusion.[5] If a person wishes to be set apart from the crowd, communication proficiency is essential.

The notion that speaking ability adds to one's professional value is as old as it is true. Demosthenes, Pericles, and Cicero are not the only ones who rode communication talent to the heights of achievement. As his greatest investment, Warren Buffett cites the check he wrote for a public speaking course during his days as a young stock adviser. Today, he evangelizes the practice of public speaking training to business students at top universities. At Columbia University in 2009, he declared, "You can improve your value by fifty percent just by learning communication skills — public speaking." To anyone willing to commit to such training, he wryly offered $150,000 in return for 10 percent of their future earnings. To those unwilling to commit to communication training, he offered only $100,000.[6]

And yet — *cruel fate!* — the skill professionals most need is the one they most fear. For every survey that confirms the demand for able communicators, another survey reveals public speaking to be among the most prevalent of human phobias. Take, for instance, the findings from a Chapman University study, which was later published in the *Washington Post*. At the top of the list of human fears was public speaking. Lower on the list? "Heights," "snakes," "drowning," "blood/needles," "flying," "darkness," and others.[7] On some surveys, public speaking comes in above "death"! In other words, researchers find that Americans spend more time fretting over speaking in public than they do fretting over just about any other common fear.

There is another, equally puzzling problem though. The available training resources, especially those that are promulgated in college classrooms across the country, routinely ignore the research that shows *how* communication should be taught. Today's public speaking instructors focus most of their attention on content creation and organization rather than on the delivery practices so lacking among today's professionals and public leaders.[8] People are largely driven by nonlinguistic signals, and they tend to do business with people they like and trust.[9] Bear in mind, though, that being liked is not about becoming drinking and gossip buddies, nor is it about being the office pushover. In professional contexts, being liked is about being relatable and trustworthy; and as author Rohit Bhargava affirms, its "ROI," or return on investment, is considerable.[10] Communication that earns trust and liking is less of a mystery than most people may think. Competent communicators are not wizards; like Demosthenes, they are people who apply a set of surprisingly basic skills.

As a professor of rhetoric and a professional communication coach with two decades of experience in and out of the classroom, I study soft skills from both an academic and a "real-world" perspective. I have prepared this volume to reflect only those skills that can be learned with minimal effort but have maximum impact. I have deliberately chosen the less-is-more approach because I believe motivated readers need only a few points of instruction to move themselves ahead of the competition. When Will Strunk penned his famously pithy volume *The Elements of Style*, E. B. White claimed the book's goal was to "cut the vast tangle of English rhetoric down to size and write its rules and principles on the head of a pin."[11] Though I cannot promise a volume on the head of a pin, I am motivated by the same aversion to lengthy textbooks, especially those that falsely promise to be succinct. Sitting on my desk even now is a 350-page, small-print manual that calls itself a "pocket guide"!

There are two general audiences for this book. The first is the large population of professionals (and the organizations that employ them) who want to improve workplace interpersonal communication and formal presentations—whether those presentations are simple territory reports or full-blown proposals for major expansion. The second audience comprises professors (and the students who learn from them) whose courses regularly require presentations but who have not been trained to teach presentation skills. Neither of these two groups has time for hundreds of pages of Byzantine lessons and assignments, yet both groups need a basic framework for preparing and evaluating presentations. This guide offers that framework.

The book is organized into five short chapters and one final chapter that is practically a fragment. Each of the five main chapters introduces three skills related to the topic of the chapter. Each chapter also includes a rubric that enables the three skills to be affirmed and evaluated in workshop or classroom settings. Finally, each chapter provides a small set of application exercises that can be practiced virtually anywhere, anytime, including in a class or team meeting. The book's skills are then streamlined into master rubrics (included in the appendix), which are simple to customize for training programs and college courses regardless of subject area.

PART I
MESSENGER

Chapter 1: The Mind

Think the Part

- Skill 1: Preparation: How to Plan for Success
- Skill 2: Visualization: How to Imagine Success
- Skill 3: Expectation: How to Define Success

One thing must be made clear from the outset: presentation anxiety does not vanish with training and experience, and that is a good thing. Research shows time and again that some nervousness produces concentration and dynamism, the very states of being for which effective presentations call.[12] The key to managing anxiety, then, is not to get rid of it but to harness its energy in order to optimize one's performance.

Consider those who perform for a living. Broadway actors, Olympic athletes, and world-class musicians do not expect to be relaxed; they are anxious to succeed, and they have learned to embrace that energy in a productive way. Presenters, too, are performers, but this role seems lost on most of them. Professionals and students alike routinely say they "just want to feel comfortable giving a presentation," as if anyone should feel cozy and snug on a public stage. If the goal is to feel more at home, one may simply stay at home, perhaps in pajamas, and let others have the opportunity to speak. Effective communication is a worthy challenge that ambitious people embrace. One need not approach every meeting or presentation as an Olympic event, but one should accept performance—not comfort—as the goal. This shift in perspective is at the heart of the following three skills.

Expert Experience

A College Speech Professor: Whenever students come to my office before the start of the semester and tell me they are looking

---

forward to the course because they "love public speaking" and "never get nervous," I become concerned. These are the students who are most likely to end up disappointed with a mediocre grade. Sure, they can stand up in front of a group and talk forever, but their performance is imprecise and often self-indulgent rather than focused and audience-centered. Their excess comfort damages their ability to stay focused and make strong efforts.

On the other hand, whenever students come to me early in the semester and explain they're thinking about dropping the course because they feel "too nervous," I smile inwardly. These students regularly outperform most of their peers, especially the overconfident ones. Why? Because their nervousness draws them into a state of sustained focus and energy. They prepare more effectively, practice more often, and perform better.

Skill 1: Preparation: How to Plan for Success

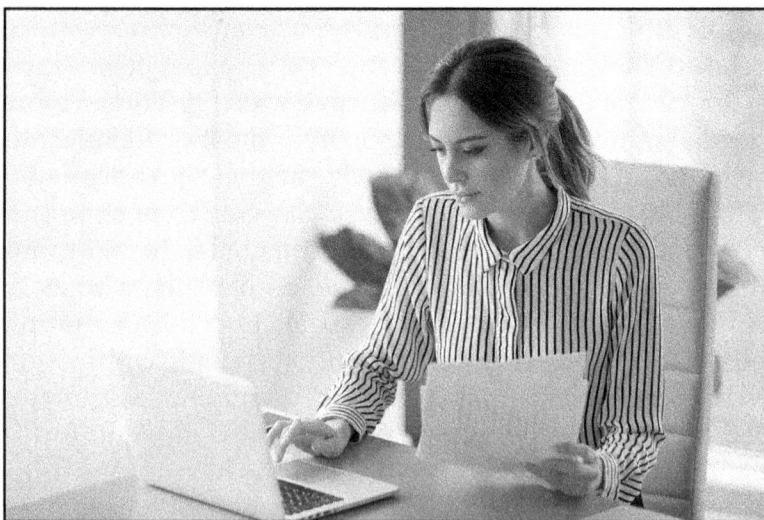

Strategy 1 – Come prepared with good content.

Being equipped ahead of time with good content transforms anxiety from insecurity-based stress into engaged excitement.

Never presume to cover up slipshod preparation with a passionate delivery style. It will come off as contrived. To the extent possible, effective communicators prepare ahead of time. As a result, they are less limited by nerves. Good preparation does not mean poring over books in libraries from morning until night, although that level of commitment would certainly pay off. With Google and any number of other research databases, it takes a relatively small amount of time to grasp the contours and key points of any topic under the sun, and even to generate a rough outline based on organization principles, such as those discussed in Chapter 4. Within an hour, an average person can go from having nothing to laying a reliable groundwork upon which to build. That kind of stability disables the fight or flight response that is responsible for most bad performances. Once a groundwork is established, schedule time for additional preparation to add research, refine arguments, and fine tune details.

Strategy 2 – Outline and memorize strategically.

One way novice presenters try to manage anxiety is to create a word-for-word manuscript to read from. The point of oral communication is to create richer human connections. Robotic, manuscript delivery disables those connections. Because adrenaline surges most during the initial moments of a presentation, consider memorizing the first 30 to 60 seconds of the introduction.[13] Because listeners will remember how they feel at the end of the presentation, consider memorizing the closing lines — the last 30 to 60 seconds. The rule of primacy and recency applies here; listeners are most focused on the presenter during the open and close of a presentation. In addition, consider memorizing or reading word-for-word transcriptions of quotations, hard numbers, or any other information that cannot be responsibly paraphrased. Otherwise, speak extemporaneously from an outline with key bullet points. In summary, do not use a manuscript, but do follow an outline, and consider memorizing or, if necessary, reading a few key parts. Perhaps the only habit worse than robotic, manuscript delivery is tedious rambling.

> *Pro Tip:* Research shows that using effective visual aids can minimize speech anxiety.[14] See Chapter 5 for advice on preparing and employing visual aids.

Strategy 3 – Stand up and practice (and practice and practice).

The third strategy of preparation is to *rehearse*. It is bewildering: when participants or students are given time to practice their presentations before they stand to speak with a camera rolling, they typically only review their content! They sit at a desk and pore over their notes. Investing time this way ensures presenters will remember a small additional percentage of the material, but they will neglect those vocal and visual resources that make up so much of a presentation's human impact.

The mind is more focused and alert when the body stands and moves,[15] which means it is easier to revise and memorize material when it is rehearsed out loud. Imagine an actor spending every free moment reviewing the script, then getting on stage the night of the performance having never rehearsed the lines. And just as an actor would do final rehearsals on set, so a presenter should try to practice in the room where the presentation will be formally delivered. At least become familiar with the environment—its size, acoustics, technology set-up, and layout—ahead of time. Doing so will minimize anxiety-inducing surprises. Building muscle memory through practice translates into fewer nerves and a more polished, natural performance.

> **Expert Experience**
> *A Lead Charge Nurse:* I had to give a presentation in a hospital training workshop. Crunched for time and crippled with nerves, I did something I'd never done before. I got up from the table where my writing had totally stalled. Standing there in my dining room, I started speaking as if I were presenting the few ideas I had to an audience. Almost immediately, more ideas came. I started

to think of new research ideas, stories, and examples I could use. Each time I added new content, I stood up and practiced my speaking again. Even more amazing, when I gave the talk, my anxiety wasn't a handicap. Of course I was nervous! But instead of feeling frozen in terror, I felt something more like excitement and energy. I have never received nearly so many compliments for a presentation. A week later, people were still telling me how smart I was.

Skill 2: Visualization: How to Imagine Success

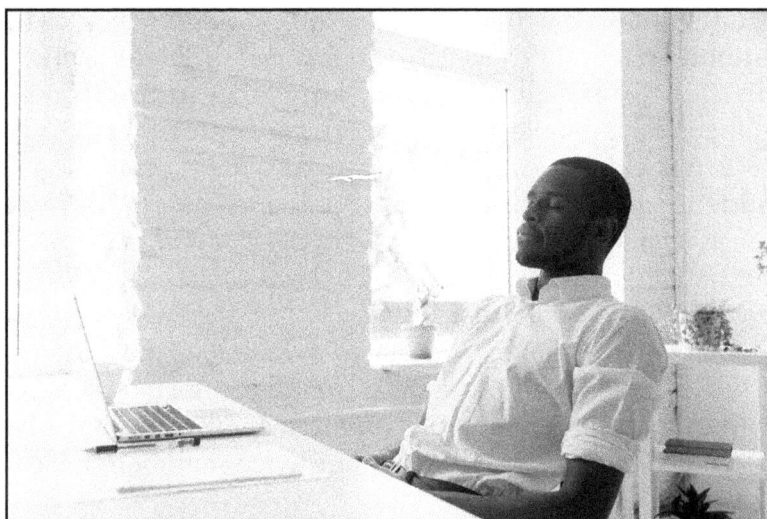

Many people have heard the saying—attributed to Henry Ford—that *whether you think you can or you think you can't, you're probably right.* Visualization research is no longer considered a fringe pseudoscience. It is routinely published in top academic journals and other reputable places.[16] It has been shown to activate the creative subconscious, build motivation and attraction, and program the brain to achieve specific goals. Performers, including world-class athletes, award-winning actors, social thought leaders, and (of course) successful presenters, use this skill routinely.

Strategy 1 – Do some body-focused breathing.

The first step in effective visualization is to close the eyes and breathe for a minute or two. Breathe deeply into the belly, not the chest, and focus on relaxing the muscles in specific regions of the body, especially the jaw and neck. This practice, if pursued mindfully, has been proven to be as effective as some prescription painkillers in terms of calming the mind and body.[17] Beware though: focused presenters are not looking merely for calm; they are looking for focused energy, which leads to Strategy 2.

Strategy 2 – Imagine specific success.

Rather than using visualization to eliminate energy and put the mind and body to sleep —a very useful talent if one can learn it—use this skill to shape the immediate future. Compose and focus on a detailed image of the successful event.

Visualize delivering key moments of the presentation in a confident way. Ask specific questions, such as, *As I deliver my message, how am I standing (or sitting)? What does my face look like? What am I doing with my hands? How loud is my voice? What am I wearing? When something doesn't work as planned, such as my technology, how am I handling it?* Relatedly, visualize the audience's reaction. Do not imagine a standing ovation after a routine team meeting, but presume the presentation's objectives have been achieved. Realistically, what do audience members look like afterward? What are they saying?

Strategy 3 – Practice positive self-talk.

The key with positive self-talk is to be aspirational but realistic. Competent, professional speakers do not tell themselves they are about to deliver world-changing orations; instead, they firmly remind themselves that they are qualified to be there. They have been asked to share a perspective because they have been deemed qualified to do so. They, not others, have been invited to the stage. It is really not a very big deal. Listeners are not expecting songs and dances. They just want a presenter who will share ideas in a clear, competent, human way. Above all, the presenter's internal voice should declare, "I'm qualified to do this."

Shift the external voice, too. Speakers who broadcast their fear of failure, or who announce that they are "bad at public speaking," sabotage themselves. It is OK—and often helpful—to confide one's insecurities in a trusted colleague or friend. However, widely sharing fears or inadequacies will accomplish only two things: (1) the presenter will be self-programed to expect failure, and (2) others will be programed to believe the speaker is unprepared to meet professional expectations.

Skill 3: Expectation: How to Define Success

Professionals do not expect themselves to be geniuses; they are more than happy with high competence. So, it turns out, are audiences. When listeners experience competence, they are disarmed, and willingly so. They want to attach themselves to capable people whom they can trust. Here are three strategies for creating expectations with competence rather than brilliance in mind.

Strategy 1 – Clarify expectations.

People with presentation anxiety are often too afraid to ask for simple clarification on what the inviter wants. Not only is it OK to seek clarification, but doing so shows initiative and responsibility. It improves the speaker's credibility with the person who assigned the presentation.

Begin conversations about expectations using statements and questions like these: *I just wanted to get a better sense of our goals for this meeting/presentation. Is it OK if we talk briefly about who will be in the meeting and what kinds of information they'll be looking for? What do you think would be more important for this audience, the territory report or the proposal for expansion we've been working on? How long should the presentation be?* If expectations have been clarified but seem overwhelming, a presenter has every right to push back respectfully and to recommend a revised set of expectations.

Expert Experience

An English Professor: Just recently, one of my students expressed disappointment in a mediocre grade she earned. When I spoke with her in my office, I learned that she was uncertain about some elements of the assignment. I asked her why she did not seek me out during office hours or by appointment to discuss the assignment. She told me that she thought she would look ignorant. The opposite is true.

Strategy 2 – Communicate expectations.

Expectations should be communicated to the audience early in the presentation. Begin presentations, meetings, and other professional interactions by stating objectives up front. Doing so not only gives listeners a reassuring sense of where the presentation or meeting is headed, it also reaffirms the presenter's sense of control. When it comes to shaping expectations, presenters tend to have more control than they think. By availing themselves of this freedom, they translate their anxiety into a sense of empowerment.

Strategy 3 – Expect problems.

What could possibly go wrong? No, really. Skill 2 above invites presenters to visualize success. They should not, however, ignore potential pitfalls. By considering various ways a presentation could get snagged, presenters accomplish two important tasks related to expectation management. First, they remind themselves that imperfect situations are normal situations – and that imperfect situations are OK. *What if there is a low turnout? What if technology doesn't work? What if other presenters go long and I am left with half of my expected time?* Such questions are not cause to indulge anxiety. They are reminders that these sorts of minor setbacks are part of the job and that as long as they are handled with a sense of control and confidence, the presentation will come off well.

Second, by considering what could snag the presentation, a presenter is better prepared to handle it. If a presenter has considered the possibility of being left with half the time originally allotted, that presenter will be able to identify parts of the presentation that may be cut or glossed over. Professional presenters respect the audience's time as sacred. They do not ask the audience to make sacrifices for them; they make sacrifices for the audience. Hope for perfect conditions, but out of respect for the audience, plan for adjustments.

Pro Tip 1: Drink room temperature water to grease the gears. Hydration is preparation. Also, there is anecdotal evidence that chewing gum immediately before (not during!) a presentation gets the muscles in gear; it also sends a message to the brain that the situation is non-distressing.[18]

Pro Tip 2: Harvard researcher Amy Cuddy argues that by privately doing "power poses" before a presentation, people can increase the hormones (testosterone, serotonin) that boost confidence and decrease stress.[19] A "power pose" is something a superhero would do. Imagine, for instance, Wonder Woman with her hands on her hips or LeBron James with his arms outstretched after a

---

thunderous dunk. Try these poses for up to two minutes before the presentation. It is not recommended that a presenter do them during the presentation!

Summary of Strategies in Chapter 1: The Mind

1. Prepare good content, and *know* it.
2. Memorize portions of the introduction and conclusion and little else.
3. Stand up and *practice, practice, practice*.
4. Breathe.
5. Imagine success.
6. Practice positive self-talk.
7. Clarify expectations.
8. Communicate expectations.
9. Plan for problems.

Application Exercises

1. Do some body-focused breathing—into the belly for several seconds and out again for several seconds. Pay special attention to relaxing the neck muscles, jaw muscles, and shoulder muscles. Notice how doing so for even a minute or two creates a sense of poise and readiness to communicate in a relaxed way.
2. Once a breathing rhythm is established, close the eyes and imagine in detail an upcoming communication opportunity. Picture its success. Imagine details, such as using confident body language and voice. Imagine the room, the sounds, and other environmental details, including the audience.
3. Identify an upcoming communication opportunity. What needs to be done to prepare for it? Even if it is a casual communication situation, craft an outline for how it should go. Given this outline, what additional information is needed in order to prepare more effectively for this encounter? Do some research in order to find that information.

4. Continuing with this upcoming communication oppor- tunity, what environmental challenges are liable to take place? Technology breakdown? Distractions? Difficult audience members? Develop a strategy for dealing with these challenges diplomatically.
5. Compose an affirming sentence that the internal voice can adopt in times of opportunity. *I am qualified to do this* may work, but perhaps something more customized would be better.

Rubric: The Mind

Mark the column that applies, note the number that applies, and provide a note of explanation if relevant.

Skills	Definitely: 4–5	Sort of: 2–3	Poorly/Not at all: 0–1
I prepared good content in advance and learned it well.			
I memorized strategic portions of my presentation, such as the introduction and conclusion.			
I practiced my presentation multiple times.			
I used breathing exercises before the presentation.			
I imagined myself succeeding in specific ways.			
I practiced positive self-talk and avoided negative self-talk.			
I avoided placing unreasonable expectations on myself.			
I clarified expectations prior to my talk, and I communicated expectations during my talk.			
I planned for potential problems.			

Chapter 2: The Body

Look the Part

- Skill 1: Stance and Movement: How to Use the Legs and Feet
- Skill 2: Gesture: How to Use the Arms and Hands
- Skill 3: Expression: How to Use the Eyes and Face

A considerable amount of the influence a speaker has on a given audience comes from just the speaker's appearance.[20] From arrival to departure, the presenter is observed and evaluated. Although audiences pay particular attention when the presentation is officially underway, they are influenced by much more than the words being spoken. Though hardly fair, research here is clear: people who look better are more successful.[21] By "look better," one does not mean sex appeal. Sex appeal may help, but it is an unwieldy, complicated thing. Instead, think of the way people visually communicate their messages and identities in professional settings. Do they *look* confident? Credible? Engaged? Professional? With the skills below, they can—no plastic surgery required.

Expert Experience
A Project Manager for a Major International Technology Consulting Company: When I encounter someone who appears unprofessional or insecure, I assume they won't be with the company long and certainly won't be promoted. I also try to avoid situations where they'd have to interact with clients because I assume the client won't respond well to them.

Skill 1: Stance and Movement: How to Use the Legs and Feet

Too much movement with the legs signals that the speaker is uncomfortable at best and desperate to leave the room at worst. Because trust is the most important resource a speaker has, it is essential that the speaker communicate stability, reliability, and comfort with the body. It is fatiguing to watch someone move helter-skelter around a room, especially if that person is also trying to share an important message. That is not to say that one should never move. Purposeful movement is good. Aimless movement is bad. The key to using the body, then, is to understand how to stand and move in a way that reinforces the message itself.

Strategy 1 – Take center stage.

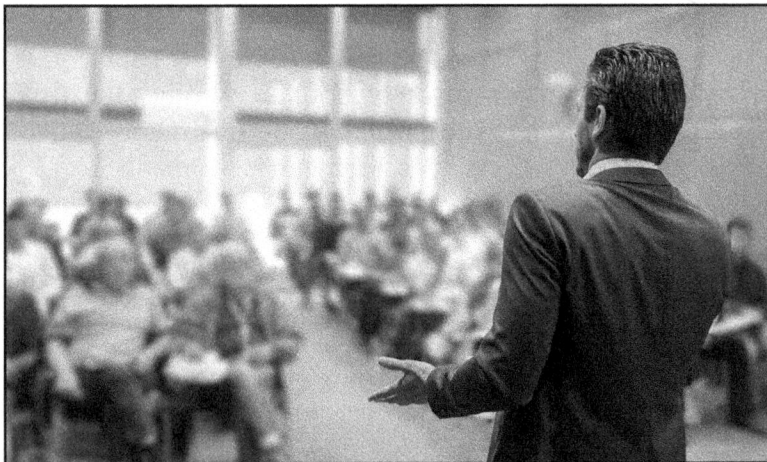

Center Stage

The presenter should be the focal point of the presentation. Under normal circumstances, the presenter should speak from the middle-front of the room—not too close to the audience and certainly not too far back. *Never* stand near the wall! Speakers who stand near walls make as if to disappear from the room. Few tendencies betray insecurity more clearly.

If the center position in the room is already occupied by a projection screen, the presenter should black it out before speaking in front of it. If it cannot be blacked out, the presenter should speak in front and directly to the side of it. Audience members find it difficult to focus when words, images, and projection lights are splashed across the presenter's forehead. In any case, maintain a position not too close to and not too far from the audience. And again, do not stand near walls.

In collaborative environments, such as group discussions and small, casual meetings, during which no formal presentation is required, it is less important to occupy center stage. Center stage is important only if the speaker is giving a formal presentation or facilitating a formal meeting.

Strategy 2 – Find first position.

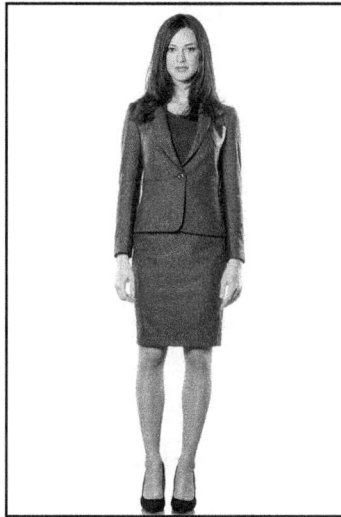

First Position

In ballet, dancers are taught a particular stance from which they begin the performance training process. Presenters, too, have a "first position." For the presenter, it is designed to signal balance, confidence, and trust. When presenters cross their legs, repeatedly shift their weight, or rock back and forth, they look unstable and nervous. At best, they come off as too casual. Subconsciously, these presenters signal their insecurity to the audience.

Stand with the legs about hip-width apart. Shoulder width

tends to be a little too wide. Stand on the balls of the feet, not the heels or toes. Balance weight evenly between the two legs. Bend the knees very slightly—no locking. Let the arms hang in a relaxed way at the sides, so the body is open. This stance will feel unnatural at first, but, performed correctly, it will not appear unnatural. With practice, it will also come to feel preferable to a closed-off stance because, on a smaller scale, it elicits the same hormonal benefits as the power poses mentioned in chapter 1. Leaving the body unguarded by cagey arm placement, the speaker will send a message to the brain and to the audience that the situation is nonthreatening. A slight increase in testosterone, serotonin, and dopamine will reinforce this feeling.

Pro Tip: Ditch the lectern. There are rare situations in which a lectern is necessary—for instance, if the presenter is in a large auditorium and no portable microphone is available or there is a formal pattern in place for speakers to use the lectern, such as delivering a sermon from a church pulpit. In such circumstances, it may appear ostentatious not to use the lectern. Otherwise, one should stand in the open. It is difficult to be an engaging speaker if one is standing behind a giant, static object and looking down at a manuscript.

Strategy 3 – Block the movement.

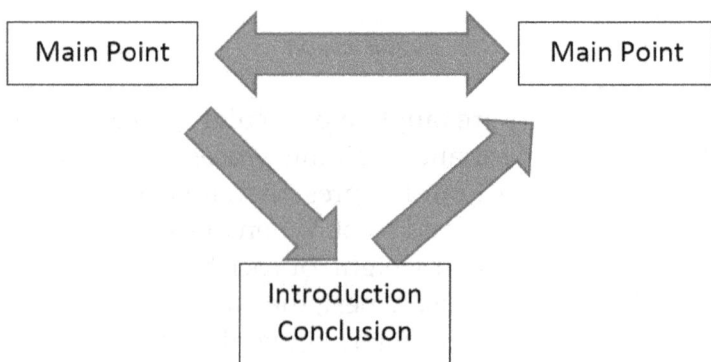

Blocking: The Speaker's Triangle

No, a presenter should not "block" movement in the sense of covering it up. Here, again, the term comes from theater. Blocking is purposeful movement. In theater, this movement is often scripted. Presenters may wish to script their movements, and some direction on this point is included below. The guiding principle for a presenter's movement, however, is simply to conduct the body in a confident way. Take several steps in a direct line, as if moving to stage left or right. One or two steps will do if the room is small. During this short walk, maintain eye contact with the audience and continue speaking. A transition in content is a good time for the presenter to move. For example: *Now that we understand the risks involved in going ahead with the proposal, let's discuss ways to mitigate those risks.* Then stop, face the *whole* audience, and plant the feet again in first position. Hold this position until another transition point is reached. Upon arriving at the next transition, walk to the other side of the room, stage left or right, and follow the same guidelines. Consider ending the presentation where it was started, at center stage. This kind of choreography lends a pleasing symmetry to one's physical delivery.

While these scripted movements are helpful guidelines, they are not commandments. So long as the presenter moves with purpose, the effect will be positive. Above all, just as one should not ramble with the mouth, so one should not meander with the body. And for the record, do not wander into the audience or to the back of the room as if to seem more accessible to the audience. Doing so will only distract and annoy audience members who can no longer see the very person they came to watch.

Expert Experience
A College Speech and Debate Coach: I've coached competitive speech and debate for years. Before coaching, I competed in it. I remember practicing the movement for my speeches: the intro is delivered from the center of the room, the first point is delivered stage left, the second point is delivered stage right, and the conclusion is delivered back in the center. And always use a good transition sentence each time you move

---

from one place to the other. My friends and I used to joke that we were going to wear out our dorm room carpet into a triangle pattern. I teach the same movement as a coach. If people do not have a way to practice confident movement, they will end up standing still the whole time or wandering around the room aimlessly.

Skill 2: Gesture: How to Use the Arms and Hands

Just as too much movement with the legs and feet sends the wrong message to the audience, so does too much movement with the arms and hands. Continuous and directionless gesturing is like a run-on sentence of the body. Amateur speakers believe this level of movement signals more passion, dynamism, and impact, but they are wrong. Such movement comes off as confusing, nervous, or otherwise distracting. Many excellent speakers gesture a lot, but they do so with purpose.

Strategy 1 – Keep gestures above the waist and away from the body.

One way to make hand gestures appear purposeful and confident is to keep them above the waist and away from the body. Watch carefully when presenters gesture. Do they gesture below the waist? Are their arms or hands still grazing their sides when gesturing? Are the elbows locked against their sides, creating a T-Rex effect when gesturing? If so, note the way these gestures seem timid and unintentional. Gestures above the waist that move outward from the body appear more purposeful and confident.

A lot of people excuse themselves by saying, "I talk with my hands." If that is the case, then why are they moving their mouths? Hand gestures definitely communicate, but if they are competing with — rather than complementing — a speaker's vocal strategies, they need to be better controlled.

Strategy 2 – Keep hands visible and open palmed.

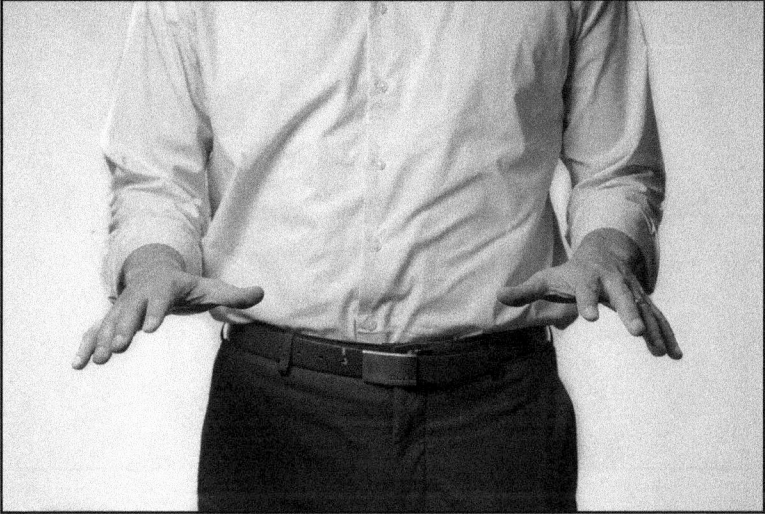

Firmness

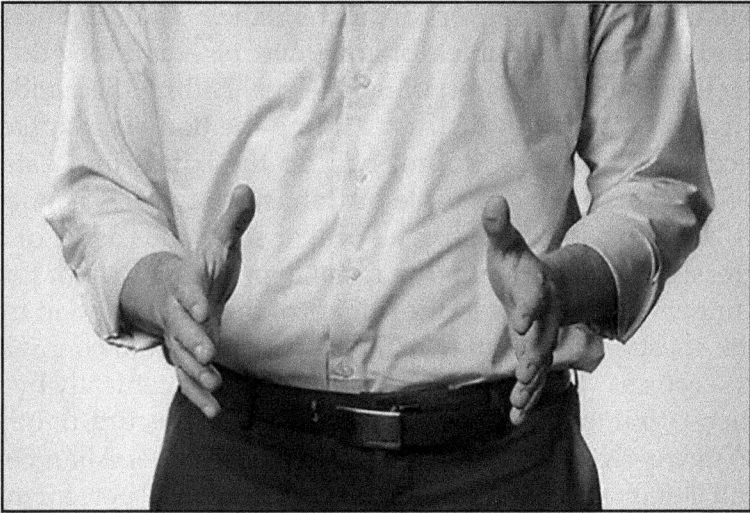

Exactness

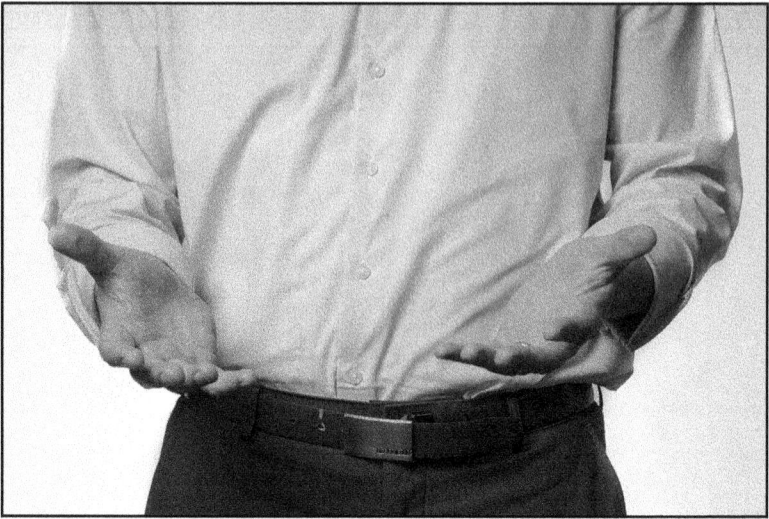

Openness

The visible, open palm is believed to be an ancient symbol of trust. Confident speakers do not hide their hands in pockets, behind backs, under tables, or anywhere else; and they do not clasp their hands in front of themselves. Hiding the hands in any way is a signal of distrust. Hiding the body is a signal of insecurity.[22] Likewise, do not ball up the hands into fists or use fingers to point at people or things. Do not put hands on hips, as doing so may make a speaker seem too casual or too aggressive, depending on the facial expression. Do not touch the fingers of one hand to the fingers of the other hand in front of the chest. Doing so may make the speaker seem conniving. Such gestures will not always be processed so cynically by the audience, but they can come across as tense, insecure, or otherwise untrustworthy. In one case study, researcher Allan Pease found that upward-angled open palms result in 40 percent more likability from the audience and that simple changes to the way palms were either revealed or concealed resulted in significant shifts in the way audiences rated a speaker's attitude.[23] There is a reason dog trainers are taught to approach animals with open palms and police suspects are commanded to show their hands. Doing so is a universal symbol that one has nothing to hide.

> *Pro Tip:* Open palms angled at about 45 degrees toward the ceiling suggest openness and welcoming. Open-palms facing each other at 90 degrees suggest exactness. Open palms facing downward to the floor suggest firmness and certainty.[24]

Strategy 3 – Practice gestures until they become natural.

Effective Example

Effective Example

Poor Example

Poor Example

It is already established that rehearsing speech delivery is key to speech success. This principle is especially true with hand gestures. Gestures that come off as robotic or forced will signal a speaker's lack of confidence, and they will distract the audience. Before applying the above strategies in a presentation, practice them more than once. As with all presentation skills, effective gesturing does not require intensive training over long periods of time. A few minutes in front of a mirror will get a speaker most of the way to basic competence.

Skill 3: Expression: How to Use the Eyes and Face

When standing before an audience at the front of a room, a speaker is essentially on stage. The adrenaline surges and the mind goes blank. So, by the way, does the face. This problem is more concerning than most people think. Without using the face's and body's non-verbal tools to communicate emotion, there is no need for a speaker-listener relationship. An email will do. But if embodied human communication is expected, the face must come to life. An expressionless face will seal the speaker off from the audience, leaving listeners bored, distracted, or confused.

Strategy 1 – Smile more (a lot more).

A person who communicates with a stone face is difficult to read. For this reason, listeners are slower to trust this person. Presenters who smile naturally and often bring a positive, human inflection to everyday life. Humans trust humans. They are suspicious of robots. But even robots can fake a smile, so bear in mind these caveats: A fake smile is as bad as no smile at all. Gratuitous smiling, for instance, could be seen as a sign of naivete or, perhaps worse, con artistry.[25] A genuine smile manifests itself easily but not constantly. It is unbridled but not cartoonish. See the application exercises below for tips on genuine smiling.

Not only does smiling send the right message to the audience members, it also sends the right message to the presenter's own mind. When the facial muscles contract into a smile, they stimulate the reward system in the human brain. Endorphins are increased, and nervous jitters are transformed into positive energy.[26] As a result, presenters who smile are rated as more altruistic and attractive.[27] All normal people hate being told to smile, but smiling casts a spell over both the one smiling and the one observing.

Strategy 2 – Match the mood.

Joy

Anger

Surprise

But of course, no one should smile during a comment about a round of layoffs, news of bankruptcy, or any other matter related to human suffering. Of the six universal human emotions, four are negative. Match the mood of the message. A person should be able to recognize the emotional tenor of a comment, whether the comment can be heard or not.

Look over presentation content long before the presentation is to take place. Are there moments of disgust, sadness, anger, happiness, fear, or surprise? If no emotional content can be found, then the presentation—even if it is a dry territory report—should be revised to include a little more emotional nuance (see *Pro Tip* below). Once the message has appropriate emotional content, practice these parts in the mirror. Ensure the facial expression matches the tenor of the content. Would someone who cannot hear the presentation be able to discern the particular emotion?

Pro Tip: One way to ensure the face communicates more effectively is to build more emotional content into the message. It is one thing to tell the audience that the company expanded sales of a certain product for the fourth quarter in a row. It is another to share a detailed example of how that product positively impacted the life of a family in Peoria, Illinois. Watch carefully when presenters share stories or offer vivid descriptions of a person, place, or thing. Their facial expressions will likely become more animated, and audience attention to their message will increase.

Strategy 3 – Hold eye contact always.

Effective Eye Contact

Poor Eye Contact

Perhaps no other visual communication practice has been so consistently mistaught as eye contact. People have been told to look over the tops of heads, to the back wall, or at the bridge of the listener's nose, or, most commonly, to scan the room as if the speaker is a lighthouse in a dark storm. People have been told that making eye contact means doing almost anything *except* making eye contact. Yet, nothing so profoundly engages an audience and channels nerves into dynamic energy as efficiently as pure, unadulterated eye contact with individuals.

Look at individual pairs of eyes. Hold the individual's eye contact for several words or even sentences — a strict minimum of three seconds. If the person looks away, continue for a few seconds to look where the eyes were. Then, and only then, find another pair of eyes. Do not speak during a transition to the next set of eyes. Do not speak when looking down at the floor or up at the ceiling to recall information. By silently shifting from one pair of eyes to the next, or from the floor to a new pair of eyes, speakers add comfortable pauses and rhythm to speech delivery. Amateur presenters think they need to make constant noise with their mouths. Mature presenters embrace that second or two of silence as their eye contact transitions from one listener to the next.

Presenters will see remarkable results with this practice. The rate of speech will modulate to become more conversational; the voice will take on more inflection, as will the facial expression; filler words will be minimized; and volume will fill the room more effectively. With genuine eye contact, presentations become a series of micro-conversations with individual human beings. When a speaker looks someone in the eye, all audience members – not just the one in eye contact – sense that the speaker is making a confident, human connection. When this objective is achieved, virtually all other delivery skills improve. Oh, and science recently found that people who make consistent eye contact have higher IQs and, perhaps more importantly, are *perceived* to have higher IQs.[28]

> *Pro Tip:* When in a one-on-one situation, do not hold eye contact constantly. Look away every ten to fifteen seconds. Also, be mindful of cultural differences. Some cultures value eye contact differently than North American professional culture does.

Summary of Strategies in Chapter 2: The Body

1. Take center stage.
2. Find first position.
3. Move with purpose, especially during transitions.
4. Gesture above the waist.
5. Keep palms open.
6. Do not cover the body or hide the hands.
7. Smile often.
8. Match facial expressions to the mood of the message.
9. Make genuine, consistent eye contact.

Application Exercises

1. Regardless of the current room, imagine there is an audience. Find center stage. Go there and stand in first position with arms resting easily at the sides. Keep the head up and make consistent eye contact with real or imaginary audience members in the room. Speaking is optional for this short exercise, but observe how this stance increases the body's energy and the mind's confidence.
2. Stand in front of a mirror in first position, or use a cell phone to take a recording. First, make no facial expression. Then, smile a genuine smile (so the wrinkles at the corners of the eyes show). Observe how dramatically the face changes and a personality emerges.
3. Stand in front of a mirror or take a cell phone recording. First stand with the feet close together and the arms tight at the sides of the body. Gesture from this position, with the elbows locked against the hips and the hands still below the waist. Note how timid these gestures appear.

Now stand in first position with the arms resting loosely at the sides. Bend the elbows and practice gesturing with open palms above the waist and away from the body. Note how professional these gestures appear.

4. Practice purposeful movement by describing two events that took place today. Starting from center stage in first position, announce that two events will be discussed (e.g., "Over the next few minutes, I will discuss two events that took place today. The first is _____, and the second is _____"). From this position, walk purposefully—do not meander—to stage left or right. In so doing, maintain eye contact and begin to describe the first event. Arrive at a sensible place on that side of the room, plant the feet, and return to first position. Finish describing that event. Once finished, walk purposefully, maintaining eye contact and verbal delivery, to the other side of the room. Plant the feet in first position again and describe the second event. Remember, regardless of where the feet are planted, address and gesture to the whole room.

5. Practice eye contact in class by standing before the group and sharing an impromptu talk—perhaps another description of two events. It can be about anything. Recite song lyrics or the ABCs, if desperate. Have everyone in the room raise a hand. They should keep their hands up until they have received eye contact from the presenter for three full, unbroken seconds (they should count silently in their heads). Listeners may then put their arms down. Try not to speak during transitions from one pair of eyes to another. Instead, pause during that brief moment, thus adding variation to the rate of speaking.

6. Pick one of the six universal human emotions (disgust, sadness, happiness, fear, anger, or surprise). Think of a brief story—or even a single sentence—that would convey this emotion. Now tell the story in total silence—mouthing the words—to another person. Use facial expressions to convey the emotional meaning. See if the person can guess which of the six emotions was being

portrayed. Are they at least able to determine whether the emotion was positive or negative?

Rubric: The Body

Mark the column that applies, note the number that applies, and provide a note of explanation if relevant.

Skills	Definitely: 4–5	Sort of: 2–3	Poorly/Not at all: 0–1
The speaker used an open, balanced stance (first position).			
The speaker moved with purpose.			
The speaker used open, purposeful gestures.			
The speaker's facial expression communicated appropriate emotion.			
The speaker maintained eye contact throughout the presentation.			

Chapter 3: The Voice

Sound the Part

- Skill 1: Volume: How to Give the Voice the Right Size
- Skill 2: Inflection: How to Give the Voice the Right Personality
- Skill 3: Rate: How to Give the Voice the Right Energy

Skilled speakers, like singers, understand that the voice is an instrument. As with all instruments, it works best when tuned prior to the performance and when skillfully deployed during the performance. And yet, the vast majority of speakers think of their voices as content delivery machines, as though a musician would simply *say* which notes the composition calls for rather than actually play the composition with care. Just as presenters do not need to be supermodels or world-class actors in order to look the part when presenting, so they do not need the voice of Broadway singers to sound the part. For most presenters, awareness of vocal quality is sufficient to develop the right skills.

The quality of one's voice is surprisingly significant when it comes to building relationships of trust. Consider one recent study published in the *Proceedings of Interspeech*. The authors found that merely the tone of voice—not the words spoken—used by couples in therapy was a better predictor of marriage success than the opinions of the therapists themselves.[29] Another recent study found that doctors with more dominant vocal tones were more likely to be sued as compared to doctors with warmer, more open vocal tones.[30] Research in infant communication makes clear that long before humans understand words, they understand emotional messages with remarkable clarity, just by interpreting the inflections of other voices.[31] It comes as little surprise, then, that companies all over the world train their representatives on habits of tone, volume, inflection, rate, and so on.

Skill 1: Volume: How to Give the Voice the Right Size

People who speak too quietly seem timid and fragile—not the qualities one looks for in reliable colleagues or leaders. The opposite problem is equally concerning. When speakers talk so loudly that they hurt the listeners' ears or make them feel uncomfortable, they come off as pushy and abrasive, or it may seem that they are compensating for hidden insecurities. Again, these qualities are not the ones people value in professional environments. Think of the term *volume* in the spatial sense. How much can the space inhabited by the audience hold? If too loud, the voice will overflow the space and push the audience away with it. A presenter wants enough volume to fill the space in which the listeners are sitting. In addition to formal presentations, this skill applies to regular conversations, small meetings, and phone calls.

Strategy 1 – Breathe from the belly.

Breath is the fuel for strong, well-calibrated volume. Knowing how and when to breathe will help maximize the range of one's volume. Improper breathing will not only stifle volume or cause the presenter to overcompensate with a tense, overloud voice but will also raise the presenter's anxiety by triggering the fight-or-flight impulse.

Before speaking, take five deep breaths. Inhale slowly through the nose into the abdomen (not the chest!) until the stomach and rib cage expand to full capacity. This should take roughly five seconds. Then exhale slowly until all of the air is gone—again, for approximately five seconds. This exercise will induce greater composure, which will improve volume when speaking. More to the point, it will train the presenter's muscle memory to breathe properly *while* speaking.

The mistake amateur presenters make is to inhale through the mouth and into the chest while they are presenting. This shallow breathing limits one's capacity for volume and dries out one's mouth, which leads to a weaker voice. Chest breathing is nervous breathing, and audiences can often pick up on it. Instead, practice breath-controlled communication, which entails inhaling through the nose and into the belly, then speaking while exhaling from the diaphragm. This strategy takes practice to master. Start simply by inhaling through the nose and into the abdomen as a general practice, whether speaking or not. Over time, this practice will become a habit and come more naturally in speaking situations.

Here's a bonus: as speakers implement this strategy, they slow their pace and include more natural pauses.

Strategy 2 – Direct the volume to the last row.

A presenter's eyes can be aimed at any individual in the room, but the voice does not have this luxury. People are often told to aim the voice at the back of the room or the back wall. This advice literally misses the mark. Rather than modulating volume to fit the room, modulate volume to fit the audience in the room.

Quiet talkers make the mistake of directing their volume at the person closest to them, whether that person is four inches away or four feet away, and they neglect the person who is at the other end of the boardroom table or the one who is sitting in the back row of the classroom. Loud talkers make the mistake of speaking to the back wall, or through it, and they forget that there is someone just a few inches or feet away who is being blasted into distraction. The solution is to identify the farthest audience member (e.g., someone in the back row) and calibrate the volume as if to engage that person in one-on-one conversation.

Strategy 3 – Slow down and AR-TIC-U-LATE.

Slowing down naturally aids in the articulation of words, inflection of voice, and raising of volume. This strategy should be a key focus for mumblers, monotone talkers, and whisperers. When presenters slow down, they increase their own awareness of the speaking situation. Because they are not rushing through content, they are better able to take cues from the audience and the environment. This awareness helps them determine whether they are whispering or shouting at the audience, and they are better prepared to modulate volume accordingly.

The problem, of course, is that when the pressure mounts and the adrenaline surges, presenters do not even know they are speaking too quickly, quietly, or loudly. Even if they do know, they do not feel capable of controlling their speech in the moment. Articulation of words mitigates this problem. Mumblers and quiet talkers are nearly identical rhetorical twins. With practiced word articulation, they are far more likely to calibrate volume appropriately. Here is the bonus: when speakers add volume, they are far more likely to add articulation, which will help with greater inflection and personality.

Skill 2: Inflection: How to Give the Voice the Right Personality

All presenters—all people—have wanted to disappear from nerve-wracking situations. The body responds to this urge by doing its best to make itself invisible and inaudible. Presenters may cover the body with arms and hands, their facial expressions may go blank, their voices may turn into whispers, and their vocal quality may lose all sense of personality. A monotone vocal delivery style is one that has no expressiveness because it never changes pitch. As with being too quiet, a monotone delivery signals to the listener that the speaker is timid or otherwise not invested in the message.

Strategy 1 – Increase the volume.

Having learned how to increase volume, speakers can use this same strategy to address other potential deficits, including monotone delivery. For some people, adding volume is the surest way to add inflection to the voice. Developing the other skills discussed above will also add expressiveness to the voice. So, look people directly in the eyes, slow down, aim the voice at the back row, and notice how monotone delivery starts to disappear.

The various strategies outlined in this book are interrelated. By solving one delivery problem, a presenter begins to solve others. This benefit is especially apparent with vocal delivery.

> *Pro Tip:* Be wary of microphones. While they add volume, they often make the user feel even more insecure about vocal quality, leading to even worse mumbling and monotone delivery. Use a microphone only when necessary, and never assume it is a solution to vocal delivery problems.

Strategy 2 – Vary the emotional content.

Listen closely next time you hear a speaker present. When people tell an engaging story, their inflection will almost certainly become more varied and dynamic. The contrast between a list of dry facts and a well-told story is not merely a contrast in content; it is also a contrast in vocal delivery. That is why adding emotional levels to message content can be so effective in terms of delivery.

Jim Kwik, a renowned speed-learning expert—and, yes, that is his real name—put it this way: "Information plus emotion equals long-term memory."[32] Easily one of the most common mistakes professionals make is to forget to highlight the human element of what they do. A presenter need not add dramatic monologues about the death of a loved one to a simple project update; but sharing a brief story about something a client recently said or adding a simple example of how the company's product impacted a customer in that territory will trigger the speaker's voice to inflect the emotional content. The result? The presenter will become more dynamic and memorable.

Adding emotional content will also likely trigger more varied facial expressions, which were discussed in the last chapter. When presenters have more varied facial expressions, their vocal expressions are likely to mirror that same variety. Again, all of the skills and strategies interrelate.

> *Pro Tip:* So much of professional communication takes place by phone, and so much of the information people consume comes through radio or podcast. In cases where the listener cannot see a face or body, the importance of vocal quality becomes colossally more significant.

Strategy 3 – Slow down and AR-TIC-U-LATE.

Strategy 3 here in Skill 2 is the same as Strategy 3 in Skill 1. Spoiler alert: it will be the same as Strategy 3 in Skill 3. When presenters slow down, they unconsciously adopt a number of other skills. They tend to articulate more effectively, placing emphasis on important words and including helpful pauses that give the audience the time—however momentarily—to consider the meaning of those words.

Additionally, slowing down sends a signal to the speaker's brain that the situation is under control. The brain responds by relaxing the mind and body. In turn, speakers are less likely to race through the message, which means they are more likely to tailor the sound of their voice to the message. That means more inflection. The payoff is significant. When presenters slow down and articulate words, they appear and sound more confident, like someone listeners can trust.

Skill 3: Rate: How to Give the Voice the Right Energy

People who speak too quickly tend to seem insecure or, worse, dishonest. When nervous, almost everyone has a tendency to speak too quickly. A rate of speech that may seem unnaturally slow to the speaker will likely be comfortable to the listener. Research shows that, for conversational presentations, a rate of between 140 and 160 words per minute is optimal.[33] This rate is fast enough to communicate energy but slow enough for listeners to process the message comfortably. Some famous motivational speakers, such as Tony Robbins, speak at a much higher rate. Doing so is ill-advised for settings like those in which most professionals find themselves. A few presenters have a tendency to speak too slowly. They, too, will find the strategies below to be helpful.

Strategy 1 – Speak only to eyes.

This strategy was introduced in the last chapter, and it will appear again in subsequent chapters. When presenters stop trying to trick themselves and others into believing eye contact is being made, and instead make genuine eye contact for several seconds with individuals in the room, they will look and feel like they are having a series of one-on-one conversations. Their vocal delivery will take on a more conversational rate. The theory here is simple: when people are in friendly conversation with one another, they are more comfortable adopting an appropriate rate, which includes natural pauses and seeks real understanding from the listener. On the other hand, when people are sick with adrenaline at the front of a crowded room, they are eager to hurry through the message and rush back to their seat. So, embrace eye contact, and approach each pair of eyes as an opportunity to have a three-second conversation.

Strategy 2 – Script the rate into the message.

Given the opportunity to prepare the presentation ahead of time, speakers should consider the following scripting tactics to maintain an appropriate rate: (1) Vary the sentence length. Follow long sentences with short sentences, and short sentences with moderately long sentences, and so on. Make use of transitional phrases, too (e.g., "As a result, . . . " "Given the information I've just provided, . . . "). Length variety will help with both articulation and rate. (2) Script in pauses. Prepare ahead of time by noting when to pause, such as after certain ideas or even specific words have been communicated. If delivering from notes, include commands, such as "PAUSE HERE!" or even "SLOW DOWN!"

But suppose a presenter elects not to use physical notes, in which case the presenter is to be complimented. This speaker should enlist certain words to trigger a reminder to slow down. Words as innocuous as *research, strategy, data, experience,* or *asset* will work well. Avoid idioms and terms that might become obnoxious if used repeatedly. Make the given word or words into a mnemonic device by mentally attaching a reminder to *slow down* or, depending on individual needs, *speed up*. With time, each use of the word or words will prompt the presenter to check the tempo.

Strategy 3 – Slow down and AR-TIC-U-LATE.

Sound familiar? It may seem obvious that, when discussing the rate of speaking, a presenter should be reminded to slow down and articulate well, but the obvious strategies are the ones that merit the most repetition. Speaking of repetition, one of the best ways to ensure appropriate rate and articulation is to breathe properly (see Skill 1, Strategy 1). By inhaling silently through the nose, a speaker naturally slows the speaking rate and implements pauses. Also, adjust the volume to the audience (see Skill 1, Strategy 2), include emotional content (see Skill 2, Strategy 2), move and gesture with purpose (see chapter 2, Skills 1 and 2), and look people in the eyes (see chapter 2, Skill 3, Strategy 3). Any one of the skills or strategies introduced so far—and certainly all of them combined—will help to ensure a speaking rate that communicates comfort and confidence, whether the presenter feels comfortable and confident or not.

Pro Tip: Appropriate rates of speed vary from context to context. People speak more slowly in a one-on-conversation (about 120 words per minute) than they do in a formal presentation. Likewise, some cultures are accustomed to higher or lower rates of speed. It is typical in the southern US for speakers to adopt a slower rate than for speakers in the northern US. Video-recorded speech, such as professional YouTube posting, is likely to adopt faster rates than in-person communication because video recordings must compensate for the passivity of a remote audience. In other words, there is no ideal mean when it comes to speaking rates across all contexts, but in traditional presentations, most people should slow down to meet the 140–160/wpm guideline.

> **Expert Experience**
> Rowena Crosbie, president of Tero International, a popular communication training company, requires workshop participants to check their cell phone greetings and listen carefully not to the words but to the quality of their voices—volume, inflection, rate. What message is the voice sending to callers each time the call goes to machine? Seasoned, confident professionals are often horrified at the dreariness of their own voices. Instinctively, they rerecord the greeting one, two, three times until they are satisfied with the effect.

Summary of Strategies in Chapter 3: The Voice

1. Breathe from the belly.
2. Aim the voice at the last row.
3. Slow down and articulate.
4. Increase the volume.
5. Vary the emotional content.
6. Slow down and articulate.
7. Speak only to the eyes.
8. Script the rate.
9. Slow down and articulate.

Application Exercises

1. Practice volume by imagining a single person in the nearest chair. Speak for a few seconds about anything as though in comfortable conversation with this person. Then, speak as though in conversation with a person in the chair farthest away. If possible, have people sit in these chairs—or stand in these places—and provide feedback on volume. A presentation's volume should be calibrated to the second person, the one in the farthest place.
2. To find an appropriate rate of speech, read this application exercise out loud from start to finish, as though it were being delivered in a formal presentation. Use a stopwatch app to time the reading. How long does it take

to complete the whole thing? Because this exercise consists of exactly 150 words, the time it takes to complete it will be a good barometer to help determine the kinds of adjustments that are needed to ensure a good rate. If it takes only fifty seconds to complete the reading, the rate is roughly 180 words per minute, which is too fast (that is three words per second!). If it takes even fewer than fifty seconds, then slow down considerably. If, on the other hand, it takes seventy-five seconds to complete, then the rate is roughly 120 words per minute, which is a little too slow for formal presentations.

3. Pick some text to read. It can be <u>anything</u>, as long as it includes a <u>clear</u> purpose and <u>several</u> sentences. Read it <u>silently</u> and <u>slowly</u>, identifying and marking the <u>key words</u> that really highlight the <u>purpose</u> of the text. Add notes to self that identify where to pause. [BRIEF PAUSE] Once finished, read it <u>again</u>—this time <u>out loud</u> and slowly. Place emphasis and <u>a little</u> added articulation on <u>each</u> marked word. Notice how doing so <u>forces</u> the voice to <u>slow down</u>, include <u>more</u> pauses, and take on <u>more</u> personality. Using a cell phone, take a recording of this reading to determine whether the added inflections add personality to vocal delivery.

4. Consider the following sentence: *The Tigers are expected to win the championship this year*. This sentence could be loaded with any number of emotions. Pick one of the six universal human emotions (disgust, sadness, happiness, fear, anger, or surprise) mentioned in the previous chapter. Write the sentence and list the emotions on a sheet of paper. Hand the sheet of paper to a partner. With the partner's eyes turned away, say the sentence while trying to communicate the emotion you chose. Can the partner guess which emotion is being communicated? Can the partner at least determine whether the target emotion was positive or negative?

5. Think of a fairly dry message, perhaps a recent email in which basic information was shared. Read or say the message out loud. Now, think of a true story that would

add a little emotional flavor to the message. Include the story and observe whether vocal quality improves. Example message without the added story: "We delivered cookies to the neighbors last week." The purpose of this exercise is to stretch oneself to see the human interest in even the most basic messages.

6. Identify two or three nonobnoxious words that are regularly used in professional communication. Use these words as mnemonic devices to trigger an internal voice that reminds the brain to check the rate of speed.

7. Record a cell phone greeting or listen to an existing greeting. What message is the vocal quality sending? Compare it to the words being spoken. Is the vocal quality congruent with the words? Rerecord the greeting until congruency is achieved.

Rubric: The Voice

Mark the column that applies, note the number that applies, and provide a note of explanation if relevant.

Skills	Definitely: 4–5	Sort of: 2–3	Poorly/Not at all: 0–1
The speaker maintained a volume appropriate for the size of the audience.			
The speaker maintained an appropriate rate of speed.			
The speaker articulated words clearly.			
The speaker's inflection added personality to the speaker's message.			

PART II
MESSAGE

Organize the Message

- Skill 1: Parts: How to Create a Beginning, Middle, and End
- Skill 2: Patterns: How to Arrange the Body of the Message
- Skill 3: Connections: How to Use Previews, Reviews, and Transitions

Few presenters are more vexing than those who ramble or habitually digress from the topic, or never even make clear what the topic is. Conversely, few presenters are more refreshing than those who communicate with structure and clarity. As affirmed in chapter 1, it is important to manage expectations by establishing a clear objective right up front. Then, impose structure on the message by dividing it into logical parts, usually no more than three. Doing so not only adds clarity to the message, it also makes the presenter seem more confident.

Most people have found themselves in one of those impromptu arguments in which they begin a rebuttal with the words, "First of all . . ."—yet they have no "second of all" in mind. Still, they use these words with great force because, whether consciously or not, speakers and listeners alike trust the appearance of orderly content. It conveys credibility. This chapter introduces simple ways of organizing a message and discusses how structural elements can maximize persuasive impact.

Skill 1: Parts: How to Create a Beginning, Middle, and End

While in artistic pursuits structure can be undermined or reimagined, practical pursuits continue to rely on certain conventions. Professional speakers commit to structure, even if all they can do is craft a discernable beginning, middle, and end—also known as an introduction, body, and conclusion. These three timeless elements may seem obvious, but a distressing number of presenters forget to rely on them. Here are some tips for establishing each of these three parts.

Strategy 1 – Use the introduction (beginning) to establish trust and reveal objectives.

Establishing trust means cultivating an atmosphere favorable to the presenter. If appropriate, tell a humorous story. Just keep it brief and relevant to the occasion. Find some reason to compliment the audience, even if it is simply, *Thank you, everyone, for coming. I know it's a busy time of the quarter.* In some cases, a well-chosen quotation may work to capture the audience's interest. Just be careful not to use something hackneyed. In short, select a simple means to break the ice.

Perhaps the most important factor in establishing trust is to show enthusiasm for and credibility with the topic. This can be done without egotism. A speaker might share some personal background and research experience related to the subject. Presenters should not brag about accomplishments or share details unrelated to the matter at hand.

Second, be clear about the purpose of the presentation and the main points that will be covered. *I am here to discuss recertification—specifically, why, when, and how to go about it.* Relatedly, let listeners know how the topic has a direct or indirect impact on their interests. *Recertification can seem like a time-suck, but it plays a direct role in how we are evaluated for raises and promotion. Plus, it ensures we are providing the highest-quality service in the industry. So, in the long run, it's good for both us and our clients.* This presenter might then share a cautionary or inspirational tale of someone whose career was impacted by recertification.

Just do not tell a story about someone whose identity might be guessed by the listeners, unless permission from that person has been granted.

Strategy 2 – Use the body (middle) for main points and evidence.

Having established trust with the audience and revealed objectives, presenters can confidently move to the body of the message. All main points should be included here. In communicating those main points, follow a simple imperative: be informed and reasonable.

Being informed means doing thorough research. Good research is objective, reliable, and recent. Mention sources during the presentation; doing so will reinforce the trust established in the introduction. Being reasonable means arriving at logical conclusions based on that research. Reasonability shows prudence and respect for the audience, including members of the audience who may disagree with the ideas expressed in the presentation. The best presenters often find ways of satisfying alternative viewpoints by offering win-win proposals. Where a win-win approach is not possible, reasonable presenters refute opposing viewpoints with courtesy.

A caveat: neither the trust established in the introduction nor the emotional tenor struck in the conclusion (discussed below) will be of use if the presenter is not well-informed and able to make sense. As St. Augustine said, "Eloquence without wisdom is generally a great hindrance, and never a help."[34] Never assume a well-organized speech will compensate for slipshod research and poorly supported claims. Gather knowledge. Be reasonable. *Then* rely on a strong introduction and memorable conclusion.

> *Pro Tip:* Use a variety of sources: statistical data, hands-on demonstration, authoritative testimony, personal experience, research studies, and so on. By showing not only a lot of evidence but also that the evidence comes from various, reliable places, a presenter demonstrates high credibility.

Strategy 3 – Use the conclusion (end) to review objectives and appeal to emotions, perhaps with a story.

Like it or not, people make decisions based on the way they feel or whom they trust more often than they rely on the facts presented to them. In professional settings, refrain from tragedian monologues and stand-up comedy routines, but embrace warm or humorous stories that reinforce key points.

A 2006 experiment conducted by *New York Times Magazine* journalist Rob Walker began with him purchasing two hundred objects from eBay.[35] Each object was purchased for roughly one dollar, for a total of around $200. Writers were then hired to produce a unique story, something very brief, for each object, which would be used in reselling the object—again, on eBay. The two hundred objects, each now tied to a story, were resold for a grand total of $8,000, a 4,000 percent increase! Eye-popping as those numbers are, they reinforce what most people instinctively know. When chosen and told well, stories trigger emotions, and emotions undermine the listener's skepticism. When moved by a story, audiences are less critical of the details. Politicians and religious leaders have long known this principle. Business leaders and other professionals have caught on as well.

While stories can be placed anywhere in a presentation, they can be especially powerful near the end. Consider pairing the story with a straightforward review of the presentation's objective and main points. If appropriate, include a call to action, even if it is something as modest as, *I hope this presentation has provided some clarity on our recertification guidelines. I would invite you to get in touch with me at this email address in order to get the process started.*

Skill 2: Patterns: How to Arrange the Body of the Message

Chapter 2 pointed out that humans trust visual symmetry. They also trust message symmetry. Almost any textbook on public speaking will provide a long list of organizational patterns from which to choose. And yet, most professionals have little time to reflect on why they might want to adopt one pattern over eight or ten others. What most presenters—and, more importantly, most audiences—need is any discernable structure at all. In short, no rambling!

This skill identifies three patterns that allow for the most ease and utility. These patterns can be applied in any communication context, from an impromptu conversation with a friend to a one-on-one job interview with a potential employer to a keynote address at a large conference.

Strategy 1 – Consider a topical pattern.

The topical pattern of organization is the most flexible. It divides messages into multiple topics of focus—they could also be called *categories* or *points* or *parts*. A speaker who would emphasize different areas of focus within a topic, or different reasons for a course of action, uses a topical pattern. *Two factors for microbial life on Mars. Three features of the Boeing 737. Three reasons we should expand into the commodities market.* Each of these examples represents a topical approach to organization. Note that the final example suggests a persuasive objective. While the topical pattern lends itself easily to informative messages, it is adaptable to all communication contexts. It is perfect for impromptu situations, too, such as when a person is asked to comment on a substantial issue with little notice. Question: *What should I know about moving to Iowa?* Answer: *I'd say there are three things to consider: the economy, the culture, and the weather.* Question: *What makes you a good fit for this company?* Answer: *Two things primarily: I share the company's long-term goals, and I am committed to its culture.*

Do not overthink this pattern. It is as simple as it appears, and it is the foundation of all communication structure: division into logical parts. Make it a habit to break all important messages into two or three main points.

Strategy 2 – Consider a chronological pattern.

A chronological pattern structures messages according to a sequence of events, moving from start to finish. It is effective at rendering complex events or processes into plain steps. Lincoln's Gettysburg Address, for example, uses a chronological pattern to help listeners see beyond a vast and paralyzing civil war: "Four score and seven years ago" the nation was founded on certain principles; now it is embroiled in civil war; recommitment to the founding principles will ensure an eternal future. Furniture assembly instructions use a chronological pattern to create order out of DIY chaos: Step 1 leads to Step 2 leads to Step 3, and so on. A CEO uses a chronological pattern to inspire employees, describing the company's humble beginnings, promising present, and limitless future. A pathologist uses a chronological pattern to help a patient understand a complex disease, explaining its progression from infection, to incubation, to manifestation, treatment, and prognosis.

Culture has conditioned most human beings to see life in terms of beginning, middle, and end. Take advantage of this conditioning. Presentations that follow a chronological pattern seem like stories, and as this chapter's Skill 1 makes clear, audiences love stories.

Strategy 3 – Consider a persuasive pattern.

Any pattern can be considered persuasive, but some patterns are consciously designed to be persuasive. Chief among them is the problem-solution pattern. It is designed to motivate listeners to change their attitudes, beliefs, or actions with respect to a given issue. Perhaps there is a problem that needs solving or an opportunity that needs taking. The audience should feel a measured sense of anxiety about current circumstances. Do not deluge them with dramatic, dishonest fear appeals, which they will see right through. Instead, provide a reasonable, evidence-based argument that a change will help them achieve greater abundance or avoid losing existing comforts.

First, define the problem and its cause. Think in terms of quantity and quality. Quantify a problem by providing reliable data on the number of people and demographic groups who are or will be impacted. Offer numbers on financial costs, hours lost, and lives impacted. Then, qualify the problem by describing how it has impacted specific people. For example, if demonstrating the need for a better mass transit system, a speaker might quantify the problem by revealing how many thousands of people are limited in their ability to pursue employment, medical care, and other resources because they do not have transportation. The speaker might then show how many millions of dollars and thousands of hours are lost as a result of these limitations. Then, to qualify the problem, the speaker might tell an illustrative story about a family for whom the problem has been significant. Here, the speaker should share details in order to take advantage of storytelling's emotional impact on audiences. By both quantifying and qualifying the problem, a speaker creates a blend of what the ancients called *logos* and *pathos*, or reason and emotion.

Once the problem is defined, quantified, and qualified, identify its cause. Any crank can point out problems. It takes a thoughtful person to link problems to certain causes. This step is not perfunctory. One of the easiest and most effective ways for opponents to discredit a presenter's proposed solution is to argue that the cause of the problem the solution purports to solve has been incorrectly identified.

If a problem and its cause have been established, and an appropriate level of emotion has been introduced, the audience will be far more likely to adopt the proposed solution, whatever it is. When outlining the solution, ensure that the proposal is (a) solvent, meaning it will effectively address the needs established in the first section, and (b) practical, meaning it will achieve its objective within reasonable constraints. If the problem is traffic accidents due to texting and driving, then a plan to incinerate all cell phones would certainly be solvent, but it would not be practical.

> *Pro Tip:* For prepared talks in professional settings that call for logistical details, consider identifying a timeline, funding source, and departments or agencies responsible for implementing the solution. In politics and religion, such details often become fodder for critics. General solutions may be better. In business, these details are often appreciated, even necessary. Know the expectations and needs of the audience, then prepare accordingly.

Skill 3: Connections: How to Use Previews, Reviews, and Transitions

Most listeners are unable to appreciate the logical links between ideas. Include small cues, such as previews, reviews, and transitions, to ensure all parts hold together in a discernable way. By including these connective tissues, a presentation not only holds together with more symmetry and strength, it also provides mechanical cushioning that makes movement from one part to the next more pleasing to the listener.

Strategy 1 – Use previews to give listeners an early sense of direction.

Once the objective has been stated and the introduction is nearly complete, provide listeners with a preview of the presentation's main points. Example: *First, I will provide . . . . Second, I will discuss . . . . Finally, I will propose . . . .* Avoid the words *firstly, secondly, thirdly,* and so forth. Consider including internal previews as well. Upon arriving at a topic that calls for subdivisions, preview it. For example, if the second main point in the body of the message is the role of evolving demographics in a particular market, include something like the following: *When we talk about demographic shifts in the Midwest, we should focus on two key categories:* . . . In many college classrooms, previewing is also called "road mapping." Road maps, even when the driver and riders have an idea of where to go, provide a sense of reassurance. Like the metaphor of connective tissue, the principle of road mapping reminds the speaker that a listener's comfort and understanding are essential. To know there are strong links between points A and B is important.

> *Pro Tip:* Compose preview points in parallel structure. That is, make sure each part is worded using the same tense and part of speech. Bad example: *We're going to examine the company's new CRM in terms of three things: its comprehensiveness, the way it is being integrated to fit our needs, and it works fast.* Good example: *Let's examine three strengths of the company's new CRM: comprehensiveness, integration, and speed.* The second example controls the list by rendering each item as a singular noun.

Strategy 2 – Use transitions to signal turning points.

When moving from point to point within the body of the message, use a transition sentence to remind listeners where they have been and where they are going. Example: *Now that I have provided some background on the economic conditions of emerging markets, I want to discuss some opportunities relevant to our products.* Sentences like this point backward and forward at the same time, making the message's organization explicit for the listener. Smaller transitional elements are also helpful. Phrases like, *therefore, in so doing, nevertheless, although it is true that, along with,* and a host of others can be used to accentuate structure and add flow to the speech. Immoderate use of such phrases is a bad idea. Like driving directions with superfluous turns, such devices can make a speech feel circuitous and a listener lost. Or, to return to the other metaphor, too much connective tissue suggests a malignancy that weakens the body. Use transitional devices, but be discerning in doing so.

Strategy 3 – Use reviews to bring the message full circle.

Upon completing the body of the message, move to the conclusion. There, reiterate the objective and main points of the presentation. Because listeners are returning whence they started, a general reminder will do the trick. Example: *Including more skill-based learning in the humanities will come at certain costs, but if institutions are proactive, creative, and unified, they can maintain disciplinary integrity.* This statement reads like a final appeal to the audience, but it is also a comprehensive review—however brief—of the presentation's main points.

Summary of Strategies in Chapter 4: Structure

1. Use the introduction to establish trust and reveal objectives.
2. Use the body to make reasonable, well-supported arguments.
3. Use the conclusion to review objectives and appeal to emotions, perhaps with a story.
4. Consider a topical pattern.
5. Consider a chronological pattern.
6. Consider a persuasive pattern.
7. Use previews to give listeners an early sense of direction.
8. Use transitions to signal turning points.
9. Use reviews to bring the message full circle.

Application Exercises

1. Select a topic and objective. Perhaps this topic is relevant to an upcoming meeting, presentation, or pitch. Identify an organizational pattern that best suits the objective.
2. Keeping with this topic or a different one, and without necessarily writing or rewriting an entire presentation, prepare an introduction that establishes trust with the target audience and provides a clear preview of what the remainder of the presentation will cover.
3. Considering the chosen organizational pattern, identify the different parts of the body of the message. If it is topical, what are the two or three topics? If it is chronological, what are the historical stages that will be highlighted? If it is persuasive, what are the problems and causes, and how will they be quantified and qualified? Relatedly, what plan will be proposed as a solution?
4. Practice writing transition sentences from point to point within the presentation.
5. Given the presentation objective, identify a number of

sources that will provide reliable evidence to support the presentation's claims. Identify which part of the presentation each source will fit into.

6. Identify a true story that captures an appropriate emotional appeal for the presentation. Consider the close details of this story; determine whether the story would fit well within the conclusion or somewhere else.

Rubric: Structure

Mark the column that applies, note the number that applies, and provide a note of explanation if relevant.

Skills	Definitely: 4–5	Sort of: 2–3	Poorly/Not at all: 0–1
In the introduction, the speaker established trust and revealed objectives.			
In the body, the speaker used a sufficient number and variety of reliable sources.			
In the body, the speaker made reasonable arguments that followed from the evidence.			
In the body, the speaker used a clearly discernable organizational pattern.			
In the conclusion, the speaker made an appropriate emotional appeal and reaffirmed presentation objectives.			
Throughout the presentation, the speaker used previews, reviews, and transitional devices.			

Chapter 5: Visual Aids

Complement the Message

- Skill 1: Composition: How to Design Visuals
- Skill 2: Presentation: How to Interact with Visuals
- Skill 3: Materiality: How to Use Tactile Visuals

While it has become somewhat trendy to criticize visual aid software like PowerPoint and Prezi, the core research has not changed. Most people are visual learners.[36] Dr. Lynell Burmark's work shows that words are processed in the short-term memory, whereas images lodge in the long-term memory. But retention is not the only benefit. Comprehension improves as well. One study argues that humans process visuals roughly 60,000 times faster than they do words.[37] Robert E. Horn of Stanford University explains that "visual language has the potential for increasing 'human bandwidth'—the capacity to take in, comprehend, and more efficiently synthesize large amounts of new information."[38] One study by the University of Minnesota found that the use of visual aids leads to a 43 percent increase in persuasiveness and, remarkably, a 26 percent increase in the amount of money potential clients or customers are willing to pay for a given product.[39] Studies or no studies, it is clear to most people that visual aids are powerful tools. They deploy messages more quickly, enhance comprehension, trigger emotion, and improve memory.

Most amateur presenters think that simply having the visual aid equips them with all of the promised advantages. Even today, many highly qualified professionals think of PowerPoint slides as glorified speaking notes. In order to project credibility and secure the benefits, create visual aids with the following skills in mind.

Skill 1: Composition: How to Design Visuals

How to use Sensory Learning to Your Advantage

Benjamin Franklin said, "Tell me and I forget. Teach me and I remember. Involve me and I learn."

- Use a material visual, such as a touchable object, a white board drawing, or a detailed handout.
- If using a whiteboard, write or draw in silence, let the audience absorb what is being prepared, then turn back to the audience and discuss the information.
- Create or distribute the visual, let the audience absorb its contents in silence for a moment or two,

- If providing food and drink, a presenter might invite participants to enjoy the refreshment in groups as they discuss a key question related to the presentation.

Crowded, Presenter-centered

4: SENSORY LEARNING

- Group Discussion
- Tactile Visuals
- Food and Drink

Simple, Audience-centered

Think of it this way: some clothing seems designed to obscure or outshine the body that wears it, but well-designed clothing highlights the natural beauty of the body. It gives structure and emphasis to what is already there and simply wants framing. Think of the message as the body and the slide deck as a simple but elegant ensemble. Here is another metaphor, more suited to the notion of performance: think of the visual aid as part of the stage and set. It certainly plays a role, but it is not meant to overshadow the actors or the script. For this reason, slide presentations should not be regarded as content delivery methods. Even when including data-rich graphics, presenters should treat them as accessories. They should be neat and graceful, not garish or distracting. Remember, the purpose of each slide is simply to add visual, graphic, or organizational clarity to the presentation.

Strategy 1 – Use text sparingly; follow the Rule of Three.

Do not write full sentences, let alone paragraphs! Instead, use words only as topic headings or in short bulleted lists. When creating a bulleted list on a slide, remember the standard of three: a rough limit of three bullet points per slide and a rough limit of three words per bullet. This guideline, sometimes called the Rule of Three, can be ignored from time to time, but it should be every presenter's default standard.

Strategy 2 – Use high-definition images and graphics.

When people recall memories from their youth, or even from last week, they probably do not recall specific words and letters. Rather, human beings tend to recall images, scenes, tableaus. Looking back on their elementary school years, adults probably cannot recall what they read in textbooks or heard from the teacher, but they can almost certainly recall what the classroom looked like, what kinds of clothes the teacher wore, and how the desks were designed.

Make slides visually potent by pairing minimal text with professional, high-definition images that add emphasis to the topic being discussed. Avoid images that might be considered inappropriate. When discussing data, use simple graphics that add clarity and elegance to the information being shared. Avoid graphics with too much information.

Strategy 3 – Embrace color and negative space.

Use color, and use it strategically. Color studies is a growing subfield of research with some reliable data.[40] Blue is often associated with calm and competence, whereas red is associated with excitement and dynamism. Green tends to be associated with growth and healing.[41] Determine what kind of message will impact the audience most effectively and what kinds of colors should be used to send it. Additionally, just as one would avoid copious amounts of text, so one should avoid garish palettes. A presenter certainly wants some contrast in the color strategy, but too many colors are overwhelming. Have a consistent color strategy.

Apply a standard of simplicity by embracing negative space. Many people decorate their homes believing that every wall must be covered and every room furnished from front to back. But most people find an open layout to be calming, as long as it is organized; so it is with slides. If colors are used strategically, negative space on a slide will add to the clear, unruffled style a presenter wants to project. A cramped slide suggests a cramped presenter.

Above are two visuals. The second one is more effective for a well-prepared presenter. It starts with a conservative but clear color palette (see the back cover of the book for the color version), which uses contrast between gold, white, and a muted charcoal. The slide uses an image with high-impact colors as the focal point. The overall design embraces negative space, and what little text there is follows the Rule of Three.

Expert Experience

A CEO: We had two final candidates for a VP position. They each gave a presentation to the board. They seemed totally equal in every way. The first presenter, though, had a Power-Point presentation that was just way too busy. He seemed to be trying to be a little too cute. He included lots of visuals on each slide, too many graphs. He even included the company logo in a rather large font on each slide, which seemed like a good idea at first. But the second candidate had a much more disciplined and conservative PowerPoint. Each slide was really sleek and easy to look at. I thought I had liked the first presenter's use of the company logo, but the second presenter just used the company colors as a background. It was really subtle but really smart. I liked it. He ended up getting the job, not necessarily because of the color thing. But every time I look back on the PowerPoint he used, I think it seemed really mature.

Skill 2: Presentation: How to Interact with Visuals

Effective Presenting of Visual

Effective Presenting of Visual

Ineffective Presenting of Visual

This skill was also discussed in chapter 2 (see Skill 1, Strategy 3). In theater, actors use "blocking" to train their bodies to move around the set in effective ways. On stage, there are certain ways to interact with the set so as to emphasize rather than distract from the performance. Most people have watched—or been— the presenter who spends the first ten minutes floundering with the technology, usually only to pull up a slide deck that was not helpful to begin with. Most people have watched—or been—the presenter who leaves a slide up long after transitioning to new information. Most people have watched—or been—the presenter who stands directly in front of the projection light as if no one will notice the images splayed across his or her forehead. Presenters who see themselves as performers, even modest performers, can avoid such pitfalls by using the following strategies.

Strategy 1 – Make the audience, not the visual, the speaker's focal point.

This strategy is overlooked by most presenters. When a slide comes up, or when something is written on the whiteboard or any other visual object is introduced into the presentation, the presenter naturally diverts eye contact from the audience and begins speaking to the visual. The most novice presenters turn their backs on the audience and read from or speak to the visual they are presenting. Just as visual aids are not speaker notes, so they are not the audience. A presenter should speak neither from nor to the visual aid.

This strategy is actually simpler than most people think. One tactic presenters should embrace is to open the slide and wait a second or two in silence while the audience takes it in. The presenter may feel free to observe the slide in silence as well. After a second or two, the presenter may then resume eye contact with the audience and begin talking. This tactic should also be used when the presenter is writing on a board or presenting any other object (see Strategy 3 below). Presenters may feel uncomfortable with a moment of silence as they look at a slide, but doing so is perfectly acceptable. In fact, it is a good way to cultivate a comfortable pace and provide more opportunities for everyone to grasp the message.

Strategy 2 – Make the speaker, not the visual, the audience's focal point.

An ideal presentation environment includes a projection screen or whiteboard at a slight angle to one or both sides of a room. Most classrooms, boardrooms, and auditoriums install the projection screen or whiteboard directly in the middle of the room. This arrangement makes the presenter seem like an accessory to the visual, not the other way around. If there is no way to alter this arrangement, certain tactics can help redirect the audience's attention to the presenter. One of the most underutilized tools is the blackout key, typically the "B" key. As soon as the image or information on the screen is no longer useful, presenters should black it out so the audience's attention returns to them.

This tactic is imperative if the presenter wants to speak from the middle of the room (i.e., center stage) or when the presenter wants to cross from one side of the room to the other. It is never professional to walk or stand in front of the projector. Instead, black out the screen, stand in the middle of the room or move to another part of the room, continue talking through the point, then bring up the next slide when ready.

Strategy 3 – Remain in control and independent of the visual.

Few things induce more speaker anxiety than technology breakdowns. Before the presentation, speakers should ensure their technology is compatible with the room's technology. Troubleshoot the projector, connectors, adapters, and controls. Still, Murphy's Law ensures that technology problems will arise, often at what seems like the worst possible moment. The show must go on. Technology breakdowns should never be cause for cancellation or even postponement, and they surely do not merit a series of excuses and apologies from the presenter. Just move on. Start on time. Technology can be retested during a short break or discretely by a colleague once the presentation is underway. Because the purpose of the visual aid is simply to frame the message in an interesting way, a presenter should be able to speak without it—the same way a good actor would persevere whether there are set problems or not.

To prepare a presentation independent of the visual aids, take the following measures. First, bring hard copies of any essential visuals that might be used as handouts. These may include graphs, charts, or tables of information that call for extended discussion. Second, for presenters who rely on slides to stay on topic and organized, bring a printed copy of the slide deck. Do not hold the pages during the presentation, but place them somewhere close and feel free to glance at them in silence as needed. In such cases, the presentation may not look as polished, but at least it will be viable, and the presenter will avoid the awkwardness of telling the audience the presentation is delayed. Listeners will admire the presenter's flexibility and control.

> *Pro Tip:* Presentation-software programs tend to include all sorts of bells and whistles that seem attractive to the amateur presenter. Limit the use of fancy transitions, animations, word art, and other distractions when designing slides. Likewise, when presenting slides to the audience, do not use laser pointers or other gadgets that may or may not work in the moment they are needed. Besides, if a slide is so complicated as to need dissection with a laser, it is probably not designed effectively.

Skill 3: Materiality: How to Use Tactile Visuals

Getting people involved in the presentation is one of the most overlooked ways of effectively persuading them to a point of view. This skill is especially useful for tactile learners, which most human beings are. Many of the benefits of the *learning-by-doing* principle can be gained just by using everyday visual tools in a conscientious, applied way.

Strategy 1 – Give visuals their own time.

In cases where a more complex image or graphic is needed, or where a more exact understanding of an idea is essential, use a material visual, such as a touchable object, a white board drawing, or a detailed handout. Follow these guidelines though: If using a whiteboard, write or draw in silence, let the audience absorb what is being prepared, then turn back to the audience and discuss the information. Do not talk to the board. If it is an object or handout, distribute it only when it is time to discuss it. Do not distribute objects or handouts early in the meeting if they include information that is not relevant at that point in the meeting. Presenters who talk over a material visual aid compete with a valuable ally.

To summarize: create or distribute the visual, let the audience absorb its contents in silence for a moment or two, then discuss the relevant details. Only then should the presenter move on. Above all, separate these more complex visual aids from the regular slide deck. Following this advice will cause audience focus and involvement to surge at key moments of the presentation.

Strategy 2 – Give visuals their own space.

Just as presenters should allow time for people to absorb the visual, so they should allow space. It was mentioned above that visual-aid slides should not be visible except when they are relevant to the content being discussed. It was also mentioned that the ideal speaking environment places projection screens and whiteboards at an angle rather than in the middle of the room. This spatial orientation ensures that the visual aid will not compete with the speaker for valuable real estate. This principle applies doubly for material visual objects.

Perhaps an engineer wants to present a replica of a machine the company is designing. Presenting this object to the audience is an excellent idea for tactile learning. It will provide clarifying and memorable interactions between the audience and the message. However, when discussion of the replica is complete, the presenter should not set it down within easy eyesight of the audience, where it will become a powerful distraction. Similarly, making notations or drawing graphics on a whiteboard or flip chart is an effective way to add tactile elements to the presentation, but cover them up once discussion has concluded and the audience has processed the key information. Slide another whiteboard or flip another sheet of paper over the image. Finally, if providing samples, whether food (always a good tactile experience!) or some presentation-related object, keep them in the back of the room or in a separate room until it is time to distribute them. In short, make sure visual objects "know their place."

> *Pro Tip:* If using material speaker notes is absolutely necessary, follow these guidelines: (1) Do not hold large sheets of paper. If possible, place the notes on a nearby surface and consult them in silence as needed. Audiences are perfectly accepting of a presenter's need to consult notes from time to time. (2) If absolutely necessary, hold the notes, but make sure they are neat, organized, and bound or stapled. Use note cards rather than full sheets of paper, which block the body and shake visibly when the holder is nervous. In formal environments, never hold or speak from a computer or phone.

Strategy 3 – Use visuals to elicit audience involvement.

Judiciously employing tactile visuals can be an excellent way to help listeners remember the message and feel more like collaborators. This approach only works, however, if presenters (a) give the material elements their own time and space, as mentioned in Strategies 1 and 2, and (b) translate the audience's attention to the object into audience involvement with the discussion.

If providing food and drink, for instance, a presenter might invite participants to enjoy the refreshment in groups as they discuss a key question related to the presentation. If sending around a replica of a machine the company is developing, a presenter should not simply allow participants to "take a look" but should invite them to observe and appreciate—or provide feedback on—particular features of the replica. And if using a handout, a presenter should direct the audience's attention to specific needs the handout addresses and what elements in particular are important to discuss. That way, participants will prepare thoughts as they read and handle the material object. When these sorts of tactile elements are integrated into presentations and meetings, listener focus and involvement skyrocket.

Expert Experience

Jeff Bezos, president and CEO of Amazon, has famously banned PowerPoint from certain meetings. In place of using a slide deck, he requires those attending the meeting to read—in silence—a four- to six-page memo detailing the relevant information to be discussed. Readers of this book, too, may find that certain types of meetings do not call for PowerPoint. The Bezos example is a reminder that people should embrace silence from time to time, even if it causes a little discomfort. Discomfort, as affirmed in chapter 1, can be a useful tool for better performance. Small periods of silence wherein audiences are drawn to a visual or some other object are excellent ways of keeping focus on the message. When listeners are directed to consider more closely the elements of the message, they are more likely to elaborate on the message, which means they become more invested and active.

Summary of Strategies in Chapte 5: Visual Aids

1. Make slides visual and graphic, not textual.
2. Use the Rule of Three.
3. Embrace color and negative space.
4. Make the audience, not the visual, the focal point.
5. Make the self, not the visual, the audience's focal point.
6. Remain in control and independent of the visual.
7. Give visuals their own time.
8. Give visuals their own space.
9. Use visuals to elicit audience involvement.

Application Exercises

1. Take a single slide from an existing slide deck. Redesign the slide with this chapter's design principles in mind:

visual/graphic emphasis, Rule of Three text, strategic color, and negative space.

2. Similar to the first application exercise, take a single existing slide, then divide its contents into two to four separate slides, each designed with this chapter's design principles in mind.

3. Using the delivery skills discussed in the earlier chapters of this book, practice presenting from these redesigned slides, using speaker notes only if necessary. Remember not to talk to or read from the slide.

4. During an upcoming meeting or presentation, look for an opportunity to write something on the whiteboard. Give listeners a sense of what will be written and why, then write it in perfect silence. Once finished, turn back to the audience and communicate the desired message or ask the audience questions related to the information on the board. The point here is to experience productive silence.

5. Alone or with partners, brainstorm some ideas for an upcoming meeting or presentation. What are some ways material objects might be used to involve the participants in the message?

Rubric: Visual Aids

Mark the column that applies, note the number that applies, and provide a note of explanation if relevant.

Skills	Definitely: 4–5	Sort of: 2–3	Poorly/Not at all: 0–1
The speaker's visual aid added elegance and interest to the presentation.			
The speaker's visual aid emphasized graphics and visuals rather than text.			
The speaker used the visual aid in a confident and controlled way.			

The speaker made reasonable use of tactile visual strategies to elicit audience involvement.			

Chapter 6: Leftovers

Brief Thoughts on Professional Style

By highlighting core skills that enable simple practice, habitual use, and long-term results, this book has deliberately left a few matters on the table. This chapter lists several tips related either to (1) reinforcing the skills discussed in previous chapters (think of the tips below as small, second helpings) or (2) filling in some of the gaps left by the above chapters (think of the tips below as light desserts). Whatever the case, committed students may find these "leftovers" useful as a means to distinguish themselves as skilled communicators.

- When practicing presentation skills, embrace the selfie impulse. Take photos and record videos during skill exercises. These selfies, of course, are not to be posted on social media. They are to be analyzed critically for personal feedback on body language, facial expression, and vocal delivery. Abundant research makes clear that the best feedback comes from presenters who watch recordings of their own habits.[42] Embrace this tool as part of classes, workshops, and individual practice.
- Tell stories. This skill is encouraged in chapter 4 and elsewhere, but it bears repeating. Stories not only add much-needed emotion to otherwise dry presentations, but they have also been shown to make audiences far more likely to buy into a speaker's message. They also play an important role in enhancing a speaker's delivery skills. When people tell stories, they unconsciously become more dynamic in their body language, facial expressions, and vocal style.

- When in professional meetings, take notes, even and especially in one-on-one meetings. Doing so communicates credibility and engagement.
- The delivery skills discussed above apply even in small sit-down meetings when a speaker is sharing a perspective or reporting information. Do not cover the body, hide the hands, or avert the eyes. Do not adopt a monotone vocal or facial expression. Just because one is sitting down does not mean one is off the performance hook. Adjust the skills as needed, but apply them nonetheless.
- Standing up straight, looking people in the eye, smiling, giving a firm handshake: these old-fashioned skills are almost embarrassingly easy to apply, and they remain effective in terms of making a good impression, yet amateurs forget about them all of the time.
- Do not overdo the skills, though. A handshake that feels like a vice grip or a smile that comes off as cartoonish will be recognized as contrived or perceived as desperate.
- Like the advice to smile often, the advice to address people by their names is almost always applicable. The use of a person's name is a sign of recognition, and it emotionally predisposes the listener to the speaker. But as with smiling, overuse can come off as insincere.
- Some good advice regarding good advice: follow it regularly, not incessantly. Know when a skill, strategy, or tactic should be modified or even ignored in order to adjust to the constraints of unusual situations. Such needs are rare!
- It is a myth that more passion is always better. While most people need to show more interest, emotion, and approachability, an emotionally excessive delivery will turn the audience off and undermine the speaker's credibility.
- Dress the way the audience expects.
- Here's a pointer: don't ever point.
- Speaking of pointing, laser pointers are not helpful. They are distracting, and if a speaker is nervous, which is practically assured, the laser pointer will show how

much the hands are shaking. Use a confident voice and empty, open-palmed hands to direct the audience's attention to visual aids.

- Speaking of laser pointers, anything that is in the hands becomes a potential distraction, and it inhibits one's ability to gesture effectively. Pens, papers, binders, surfaces, laptops, phones, and so forth. Ditch them all.

- One exception: clickers are acceptable but less essential than most people think. They also have a tendency to inhibit one's body language, gestures, and eye contact. Try practicing without a clicker. Many professional presenters have developed an easy and confident way of briefly stepping to the computer to advance the slide presentation.

- Stand even when speaking on the phone. Doing so triggers better vocal delivery. Use gestures and facial expressions, too. This skill is key for professionals who spend a lot of time on the phone.

- Use all of the applicable visual and vocal skills when on Skype or some other online platform. Sitting is OK, even expected, but find a straight-forward angle to ensure the audience's perspective is not oriented too far downward, upward, or sideways. Remember to make eye contact with the camera, not the people on the screen.

- Use active voice often:
  - "Micah invited our marketing team to . . . " rather than "The marketing team was invited by Micah to . . ."

  - "Canadian researchers discovered that . . . " rather than, "It was discovered that . . ."

- Use stylistic devices judiciously. Metaphors, similes, repetitions, alliterations, and other figures are effective in moderation.

- Use the first-person pronoun often (e.g., *I*, *we*).

- Avoid offensive language, and define *offensive* broadly. Steer away from exclusionary pronouns, presumptions about gender, stereotypes of any kind, awkward personal stories, innuendos or euphemisms, and technical jargon that would make some participants feel lost or left out.

- When not speaking, listen actively and show it. Make eye contact, use facial expressions to signal understanding, nod the head from time to time (not constantly), repeat or rephrase the question as needed for clarification, thank the questioner, and pause to think before answering.
- When watching other speakers, make a to-do list and a *not*-to-do list. Notice what habits, ticks, talents, and deficits other speakers have. What is obnoxious? What is persuasive? Create short lists to ensure good habits are modeled and bad habits are avoided.
- Three ways to ensure audience satisfaction: (1) Start and end on time. (2) Start and end on time. (3) Start and end on time.
- Start and end on time.
- Leave sufficient time for questions from the audience.
- A fourth way to ensure audience satisfaction: include snacks.
- A fifth way to ensure audience satisfaction: end a few minutes early.
- One way to ensure audience *dis*satisfaction: start the presentation or meeting late.
- A second way to ensure audience *dis*satisfaction: go over time.
- Remember, the presentation is not over once questions start. Maintain and redouble visual and vocal delivery skills from chapters 2 and 3 during the Q&A.
- A presentation is not over until the presenter is safely in the car driving home.
- Embrace natural lighting if it is available.
- Apply all possible skills in sit-down meetings, just as they would be applied in formal stand-up presentations: open body language, open gestures, eye contact, dynamic vocal delivery, and so on.
- Ensure the presentation space is clean, organized, well lit, and comfortable. For meetings or presentations that

are scheduled to go ninety minutes or more, include a short break.
- In terms of personal performance, seek professional-level competence, not brilliance.
- Be a decent person. It is an effective rhetorical strategy.
- Be a skilled and knowledgeable person. It is an effective rhetorical strategy.
- Be friendly and likable. There is nothing empowering about being brutish. *Caveat:* being a pushover is neither friendly nor likable. The best communicators manage to be friendly and likable even as they command trust and respect.
- Commit to proper grooming. Not everyone is persnickety about whether shoes are polished or nails are trimmed, but many people are. There is nothing wrong—and perhaps much right—with calloused hands and a weathered face. But poorly maintained facial hair, wrinkled clothes, foul odors, and any other disorderliness can undermine one's professional goals.
- When in the presence of a man and a woman, some men have a tendency to speak only to the other man. Some women have a tendency to speak only to the other woman. This practice is objectionable. Addressing and inviting input from each person is a sign of dignity.

Rubric: Leftovers

Mark the column that applies, note the number that applies, and provide a note of explanation if relevant.

Skills	Definitely: 4–5	Sort of: 2—	Poorly/Not at all: 0–1
The speaker started and ended the presentation on time.			

Conclusion:

The Victory of Astrid Tuminez

Having been tasked with finding a keynote speaker for a small conference on campus, a colleague and I considered a sizable list of alumni. We looked at some minor celebrities, successful writers, wealthy professionals, and others. My colleague mentioned "the new president of Utah Valley University." UVU is a large, neighboring institution that has experienced massive growth in recent years and just hired a high-profile new leader by the name of Astrid Tuminez. I had seen her on local television and in local magazines. I recalled her as a charismatic but diminutive woman—under five feet tall—with a soft voice and an unusual personal history. She came from the Philippines. Beyond these surface details I knew very little about her. As I looked more closely into her background, I learned that she spoke many languages. She has a PhD from a prestigious university and a lot of experience as an international corporate executive. As someone who could speak to our humanities majors about professional and personal success, she seemed like an acceptable choice.

Before sending an official invitation, though, I wanted to do more research. She was impressive on paper, but would she be able to speak to our students in a compelling way? Would she be able to connect her experience to the lives of our students? In short, would she be likable, interesting, and persuasive? I soon learned that Astrid Tuminez did not just grow up in the Philippines; she grew up in abject poverty within one of that nation's poorest communities—a place without electricity, running water, or even a working roof. One day, she and her sisters brought home a stray dog as a pet. It was stolen and eaten by a neighboring family that same day. I also learned that she did not just get a good education; she managed to get a full scholarship to Brigham Young University and graduate degrees from Harvard and MIT. She did not just achieve relative success in her profession; she became a high executive at some of the world's wealthiest private companies, including Carnegie, AIG, and Microsoft. How does a young, malnourished, illiterate girl in an obscure slum on the other side of the world become an international corporate executive, then president of one of the largest universities in the United States?

To bridge the chasm between poverty and prestige, Astrid Tuminez began with what she calls "the pivot," an opportunity to earn a formal education.[43] Nuns had come across her family in the urban squalor of Iloilo, her native province in the Philippines, and recognized some potential. They invited Astrid and her sisters to attend the area's convent school for free. Astrid was the worst student in her class. Barely able to write her own name, she was placed in the last chair in the last row of the classroom. Her fellow students were not only superior academically, but they also had more means. While they spent their breaks buying snacks, Astrid had few options but to go to the library and practice reading. She almost never left. Like Demosthenes's basement, Astrid's school library became a private haven for personal development. She read voraciously, daily, and for years. She soon became one of the school's top students. Her future had gone from hopeless to promising, thanks to the opportunity she was given and her willingness to study.

One could say the rest is history, but somewhere along the way, in addition to all of the reading and hard work, Astrid also learned the power of face-to-face communication. A simple look over her resume reveals a number of positions, including diplomatic initiatives to the former Soviet Union and the United States Institute of Peace, that call for skills far beyond academic reading and writing. These skills are easily observable in videos of present-day Dr. Tuminez being interviewed as a corporate executive, stumping as a university president, or giving a TED Talk on empowering women. When I met her the day she presented at our modest campus conference, I knew I would tower over her. I am six-three. The juxtaposition must have been somewhat comical. Yet, when I introduced myself, she looked me directly in the eyes, took my extended hand, and gave it a firm shake. She addressed me with a confident voice and easy smile. Even in that brief moment, and even as someone who teaches these skills for a living, I felt a surge of likability and trust in this person. She was a leader I would be inclined to follow.

Upon being introduced to the audience, the first thing Dr. Tuminez did was to ditch the handheld microphone we had provided. We quickly set up her lapel mic. The second thing she did was to step away from the lectern and stand in the middle of the front of the auditorium—center stage. She looked directly into the faces of people in the auditorium. She smiled. Her voice, though naturally soft, was not quiet, and it resonated confidently to the back row. Her gestures, open, purposeful, and confident, remained well above her waist. Her hands, too, suggested openness, firmness, and exactness with visible palms and natural, purposeful gestures. When she brought up her slide presentation, she did not read from it or stand in front of it, even though it was displayed on a massive screen directly in the middle of the room. Instead, she stood just to the side of it, directing her listeners' attention occasionally to its image-rich messages. She stated her objective early and clearly, and she pursued it with authority, logic, and just the right amount of emotion for the occasion. She included hard data, research studies, and well-placed personal stories. She never appeared flustered or excited, but she was consistently engaged and composed.

And she was a hit. The students were eager to participate in the Q&A afterward. Their admiration was clear in the nature of their questions and the tone of their voices. For days afterward, my colleague and I received compliments from students, faculty, and administrators on what a great keynote speaker we had invited and how perfectly suited she was to the occasion and the audience, and we were encouraged to maintain a relationship with her into the future. To suggest such a reaction is attributable entirely to President Tuminez's ability to stand and speak with confidence would be an oversimplification. Lots of people who are not university presidents can stand and speak with confidence. What can be reasonably inferred is that, with a ready suite of practiced communication skills, President Tuminez marshalled the whole package, coupling knowledge and expertise with performance to expand her already considerable influence in the world.

When I asked President Tuminez what kind of communication training she had sought out, she replied that she had no formal training but that she had accepted opportunities to speak throughout her life and that she sought out jobs that had an "external facing component," which meant she would have to rely on powerful soft skills in order to exert influence. She also emphasized that wherever possible, she uses stories and images to hit her arguments home. By breaking arguments down into stories and using "good pictures" in order to convey her message, she finds she is much better at "connecting with her audiences."[44] Whereas Demosthenes was moved by the shame of failure, the young Astrid Tuminez was driven by rare moments of opportunity. Willing to embrace every chance to speak, teach, and learn, she was ready when the occasion struck—that is, when showtime finally arrived.

Some readers of this book have felt a little like Demosthenes, wishing they could cover their heads and slink away from a presentation gone wrong. Others have not faced that shame, but they know the opportunity will come, and they want to be ready. Regardless of where a presenter is in terms of experience, profession, talent, or motive, the skills recommended in the preceding chapters apply equally. Choose one, maybe two, of the skills that seem most urgent. For many people, better eye contact, increased vocal inflection, or more open body language and gestures will open the floodgates of communication proficiency. Whatever the skill may be, hone it for the next week or two. Do not wait for the next presentation at work. Practice the skill at home with family members, at a restaurant with the server, or at a party with an acquaintance. There is no need to announce it. Just do it as part of life's regular interactions. Those who follow this advice are surprised at how quickly the practiced skills become habits and how naturally other skills begin to follow.

I began the book with a couple of anecdotes: one about the famous orator Demosthenes and one about the famous investor Warren Buffett, both of whom credited practice in public speaking with much of their success. Among them, Astrid Tuminez, and countless other leaders, there seems to be a common recipe. Smart, hardworking people will almost always find a livelihood, but the exceptional people of the world — the exceptional people of a company or university or any other organization — tend to be those who understand that work and education are best paired with a confident, approachable speaking style. The purpose of this small book has been to demystify effective communication by breaking it down into basic, learnable skills. Presenting well is not a mystery; it is a matter of literacy. With the right opportunities and a modicum of knowledge and practice, exceptional results can be achieved by anyone starting from anywhere.

Appendix: Master Rubrics

Although each chapter contains its own rubric for evaluating the skills it teaches, constraints dictate that having all of the rubrics handy when evaluating a single presentation will be too cumbersome. Here are two rubrics. The first is a reprint of the rubric from chapter 1, "Think the Part." This rubric should be filled out by the presenter prior to the presentation. The second rubric attempts to cover the main skills from chapters 2–6. It is the most comprehensive rubric because it covers The Body, The Voice, Structure, and Visual Aids.

Pre-Presentation Self-Audit (reprinted from chapter 1)

Skills	Definitely: 4–5	Sort of: 2–3	Poorly/Not at all: 0–1
I prepared good content in advance and learned it well.			
I memorized strategic portions of my presentation, such as the introduction and conclusion.			
I practiced my presentation multiple times.			
I used breathing exercises before the presentation.			
I imagined myself succeeding in specific ways.			
I practiced positive self-talk and avoided negative self-talk.			
I placed reasonable expectations on myself.			
I clarified expectations prior to my talk.			
I planned for potential problems.			

Comprehensive Presentation Skills Rubric

Skills	Definitely: 4–5	Sort of: 2–3	Poorly/Not at all: 0–1
The speaker started and ended the presentation on time.			
The speaker used open and purposeful movement and gesture.			
The speaker used effective eye contact and facial expression.			
The speaker maintained effective volume, rate, and inflection of voice.			
The speaker established trust, stated objectives, and previewed main points in the introduction.			
The speaker used a discernable and effective organizational pattern in the body.			
The speaker supported arguments with copious, varied, and reliable research.			
The speaker's conclusion reviewed objectives and appealed to emotions appropriately.			
The speaker's visual aids added emphasis and elegance, not clutter.			

Endnotes

1 Plutarch, in *Demosthenes' On the Crown*, ed. James J. Murphy (Davis, CA: Hermagoras Press, 1983), 5.

2 Plutarch, in *Demosthenes' On the Crown*, 6.

3 Quintilian, *Institutio Oratoria* (Cambridge: Harvard University Press, 2001), 11.3–6.

4 Pew Research Center, "The State of American Jobs," October 6, 2016, accessed May 1, 2019, https://assets.pewresearch.org/wp-content/uploads/sites/3/2016/10/ST_2016.10.06_Future-of-Work_FINAL4.pdf.

5 Caleb Benjamin Evers, "Revisiting Delivery in the Basic Course" (master's thesis, Iowa State University, 2018), 4, https://lib.dr.iastate.edu/etd/16350/.

6 Carmine Galo, "Billionaire Warren Buffett Says This 1 Skill Will Boost Your Career Value by 50 Percent," Inc., January 5, 2017, accessed May 1, 2019, https://www.inc.com/carmine-gallo/the-one-skill-warren-buffett-says-will-raise-your-value-by-50.html.

7 Christopher Ingraham, "America's Top Fears: Public Speaking, Heights, and Bugs," *Washington Post*, October 30, 2014, accessed May 1, 2019, https://www.washingtonpost.com/news/wonk/wp/2014/10/30/clowns-are-twice-as-scary-to-democrats-as-they-are-to-republicans/?noredirect=on&utm_term=.eed4efe55e62.

8 Evers, "Revisiting Delivery," 5, 60. See also Alex (Sandy) Pentland and Tracy Helbeck, "Understanding 'Honest Signals' in Business," MIT Sloan Management Review, October 1, 2008, accessed May 1, 2019, https://sloanreview.mit.edu/article/understanding-honest-signals-in-business/.

9 Michael D. Harris, "When to Sell with Facts and Figures, and When to Appeal to Emotions," *Harvard Business Review*, January 26, 2015.

10 Rohit Bhargava, *Likeonomics: The Unexpected Truth behind Earning Trust, Influencing Behavior, and Inspiring Action* (Hoboken: John Wiley and Sons , 2012), 45.

11 William Strunk Jr. and E. B. White, *The Elements of Style*, 3rd ed. (Boston: Allyn and Bacon Press, 1979), xi.

12 Katharina Star, "The Benefits of Anxiety and Nervousness," Verywell Mind, updated March 18, 2019, accessed May 1, 2019, https://www.verywellmind.com/benefits-of-anxiety-2584134.

13 Stephen Lucas, "Speech Anxiety," NCA Concepts in Communication Video Series, National Communication Association, January 11, 2019, https://www.youtube.com/watch?v=3Jk_V6wMACY&list=PLaETCkw7w_Q_OC9R2mWv7wjjIpGSfdHJc&index=4

14 "Speech Anxiety," NCA Concepts in Communication Video Series, National Communication Association, April 16, 2019, https://www.youtube.com/watch?v=JYIcq9nzFjs&list=PLaETCkw7w_Q_OC9R2mWv7wjjIpGSfdHJc&index=1

15 Ranjana K. Mehta, Ashley E. Shortz, and Mark E. Benden, "Standing Up for Learning; A Pilot Investigation on the Neurocognitive Benefits of Stand-Biased School Desks,"

International Journal of Environmental Research and Public Health 13, no. 1 (2016): 59, https://doi.org/10.3390/ijerph13010059.

16 Nino Frederico L. Arvican, Evangeline Atienza-Bulaquina, and Lucille D. Evangelista, "The Effects of Visualization on Academic Performance of College Students," *Journal of Information and Education Technology* 4, no. 2 (April 2014): 156–60. This piece cites several other studies on visualization's impact on athletes and other performers.

17 Vidyamala Burch and Danny Penman, *You Are Not Your Pain: Using Mindfulness to Relieve Pain, Reduce Stress, and Restore Well-Being—An Eight-Week Program* (New York: Flatiron Books, 2015).

18 Caitlin Covington, "Does Chewing Gum Reduce Anxiety?" Greatist, November 11, 2011, accessed May 1, 2019, https://greatist.com/happiness/does-chewing-gum-reduce-anxiety.

19 For a popular piece, see Kim Elsesser, "Power Posing Is Back: Amy Cuddy Successfully Refutes Criticism," Forbes Media, April 3, 2018, accessed May 1, 2019, https://www.forbes.com/sites/kimelsesser/2018/04/03/power-posing-is-back-amy-cuddy-successfully-refutes-criticism/#3a2ed8513b8e. Cuddy's research, once criticized, has since been reaffirmed with new layers of scientific evidence.

20 Pentland and Helbeck, "Understanding 'Honest Signals' in Business."

21 Halvorsen, 2015.

22 See Carol Kinsey Goman, *The Silent Language of Leaders: How Body Language Can Help—or Hurt—How You Lead* (San Francisco: Jossey-Bass, 2011), 26. Also see this more accessible article by Susan Weinschenk: "Your Hand Gestures Are Speaking for You," PsychologyToday.com, September 26, 2012, accessed May 1, 2019, https://www.psychologytoday.com/us/blog/brain-wise/201209/your-hand-gestures-are-speaking-you.

23 Allan Pease, *Signals: How to Use Body Language for Power, Success, and Love* (New York: Bantam, 1984). Pease also discusses his case study in his 2013 TEDx Talk, "Body Language, the Power Is in the Palm of Your Hands," https://www.youtube.com/watch?v=ZZZ7k8cMA-4.

24 Weinschenk, "Your Hand Gestures."

25 Marianne La France, *Why Smile?: The Science behind Facial Expressions* (New York: Norton and Company, 2013). See this source for a comprehensive study of the complexity and power of smiling.

26 Ronald E. Riggio, "There's Magic in Your Smile: How Smiling Affects Your Brain," Psychology Today, June 25, 2012, accessed May 1, 2019, https://www.psychologytoday.com/us/blog/cutting-edge-leadership/201206/there-s-magic-in-your-smile.

27 Marc Mehu, Karl Grammer, and Robin I. M. Dunbar, "Smiles When Sharing," *Evolution and Human Behavior,* 28 (2007): 415–22.

28 Nora A. Murphy, "Appearing Smart: The Impression Management of Intelligence, Person Perception Accuracy, and Behavior in Social Interaction," *Personality and Social Psychology Bulletin* 33, no. 3 (2007): 325–39.

29 Md Nasir, Wei Xia, Bo Xiao, Brian Baucom, Shrikanth S. Narayanan, and Panayiotis Georgiou, "Still Together?: The Role of Acoustic Features in Predicting Marital Outcomes," *Proceedings of Interspeech*, September 6, 2015.

30 Roger Dobson, "Dulcet Tones of Surgeon's Voice May Have Hidden Meaning," BMJ 325 (August 10, 2002): 297, accessed May 1, 2019, https://www.bmj.com/content/325/7359/297.2.full.

31 Tobias Grossmann, Regine Oberecker, Stefan Paul Koch, and Angela D. Friederici, "The Developmental Origins of Voice Processing in the Human Brain," *Neuron 65*, no. 6 (2010), accessed May 1, 2019, http://dx.doi.org/10.1016/j.neuron.2010.03.001.

32 Jim Kwik, Kwik Brain 001: "Learn Anything Faster," https://jimkwik.com/kwik-brain-001/.

33 Lynda Stucky, "What Is the Ideal Rate of Speech?" ClearlySpeaking, July 30, 2015, accessed May 1, 2019, https://clearly-speaking.com/what-is-the-ideal-rate-of-speech/.

34 St. Augustine, "On Christian Doctrine," in *The Rhetorical Tradition: Readings from Classical Times to the Present,* 2nd ed., ed. Patricia Bizzell and Bruce Herzberg (Boston: Bedford/St. Martin's, 2001), 458.

35 Joshua Glenn and Rob Walker, eds., *Significant Objects* (Seattle: Fantagraphics Books, 2012).

36 T. J. McCue, "Why Infographics Rule," Forbes Media, January 8, 2013, accessed May 1, 2019, https://www.forbes.com/sites/tjmccue/2013/01/08/what-is-an-infographic-and-ways-to-make-it-go-viral/#7639b9357272.

37 Karla Gutierrez, "Studies Confirm the Power of Visuals in eLearning," Aura Interactiva, July 8, 2014, accessed May 1, 2019, https://www.shiftelearning.com/blog/bid/350326/studies-confirm-the-power-of-visuals-in-elearning.

38 Gutierrez, "Studies Confirm the Power of Visuals in eLearning."

39 Douglas R. Vogel, Gary W. Dickson, and John A. Lehman, "Persuasion and the Role of Visual Presentation Support," the UM/3M Study (Working Paper Series, Management Information Systems Research Center, Minneapolis, 1986).

40 Paul A. Bottomley and John R. Doyle, "The Interactive Effects of Colors and Products on Perceptions of Brand Logo Appropriateness," *Marketing Theory,* March 1, 2006, https://doi.org/10.1177%2F1470593106061263.

41 Lauren I. Labrecque and George R. Milne, "Exciting Red and Competent Blue: The Importance of Color in Marketing," *Journal of the Academy of Marketing Science* 40, no. 5 (2012): 711–27.

42 R. G. Bankston and L. A. Terlip, "The Effects of Videotaping on Student Performances in the Basic Communication Course," paper presented at the annual meeting of the Speech Communication Association, New Orleans, LA (1994); Do Thi Quy Thu and Dang Thi Cam Tu, "Impacts of Video-Recorded Feedback in Public Speaking Classes: An Empirical Study," *Language Education in Asia* 5, no. 1 (2014): 28–45. Video feedback has been around for a very long time, and its positive impacts are well known.

43 Astrid Tuminez, "The Humanities: Your Secret Weapon for Success" (Brigham Young University, Annual English Department Symposium, Provo, UT, February 28, 2019).

44 Astrid Tuminez, personal communication, May 8, 2019.

Acknowledgments

I wish to thank Dr. Terry West, who coached me during my formative years as a college debater and platform speaker; Dr. Matt McGarrity and Dr. Leah Ceccarelli, who introduced me to the craft of public speaking as a subject worthy of academic study and teaching; and Ro Crosbie and Deb Rinner, who gave me the opportunity to translate my academic interests into applied coaching with professional clients.

About the Author

Richard Benjamin Crosby holds a PhD in communication from the University of Washington. He is an associate professor of rhetoric in the English department at Brigham Young University. He teaches courses in public speaking, persuasion, and the history of rhetoric. Above all, I thank Becca for her full partnership in life.